# RECOVERY
## to
# DESTINY

**Journey to the Promised Land**

RECOVERY

"Millions are sinking in the quicksand of abuse and addiction. Drawing from her own experience and that of others, Deanna shows how God saves us from the swamp, cleans us up and sets us on a path of freedom. Her analogy of the spiritual journey from Egypt, to the wilderness, and finally to the promised land is valid and so is her depiction of the reality of the spiritual battle waging war against our minds. If you desire to live a liberated life in Christ, you will find this book very helpful."

Dr. Neil T. Anderson
Founder and President Emeritus, Freedom in Christ Ministries

"We're all on a journey. Author Deanna Allen, in her usual encouraging and in- sightful way, challenges readers to stop and take stock of where they are on their life journey and ask themselves if they're really headed in the right direction. Using stories from the Scriptures, she helps readers see the commonality of the human condition—our hurts, our disappointments, our sins, and most of all, our need for the God who forgives and loves unconditionally—and who has a vision and plan for each of us that is full of hopes and fulfilled dreams and a destiny more wonder- ful than we can possibly imagine. Best of all, she reminds us that it is never too late to step into that destiny and begin to take our first tentative steps toward healing and fulfillment."

Kathi Macias
Award-winning author of thirty books and host of "Write the Vision"
www.kathimacias.com

Deanna has become a treasured friend and ministry partner. She is, without question, one of the most spiritually powerful women of God I've met anywhere in the world. It's an understatement to describe her as a giant of the faith. This woman could put an army of Goliaths to flight. Her insight and spiritual discernment are unparalleled. She listens to the cry of women's hearts with intensity and hears from God with tremen- dous accuracy. It is my prayer that this book will enable thousands of women around the world to benefit from Deanna's extraordinary spiritual gifts."

Donna Partow
Author, *Becoming the Woman God Wants Me To Be*

"A powerful testimony of God's redeeming grace. Deanna's journey from darkness to light is gripping. She paints a passionate Destiny for God's children to pursue."

Mel Goebel
Founder, Daughters of Destiny Women's Prison Ministry
Author, *Unseen Presence* and *The Bride Overslept*

"Buckle up! Whether it's hope you're after, or spiritual insight, or sound teaching or inspiring stories, Recovery to Destiny leaves you thinking, 'I can too!'"

Connie Cavanaugh
International speaker, author of *From Faking it to Finding Grace*

"From the madness of a life of sinful addictions to finding God's true plan and purpose for her life, Deanna Allen shares her tremendous insights in helping others to find their own destiny. This is truly one of the best books I have ever read on understanding God's power to overcome sin."

Marty Angelo
Minister & Author

"In a society craving authenticity, From Recovery to Destiny rushes to the rescue. How? With refreshing candor for Christ, it invites people into the presence of Jesus –the true Lover of our souls. Enjoy the book as you journey with Jesus! Read it. Then share it!"

Stacie Ruth Stoelting
Author, Speaker, Recording Artist, "700 Club" Columnist,
Founder, Bright Light Ministries

"Deanna Allen is a passionate woman. Her heart for our God pours out in her words, her expressions, her life. She loves people and longs for them to experience the life-saving grace of our heavenly Father. Her experiences and depth of knowledge combine to bring her words to life."

Elsa Kok Colopy
Author, *A Woman Who Hurts, A God Who Heals* and
*A Woman With a Past, A God With A Future*

"Many women have told me how much they appreciate your books. Hearts have been touched and lives encouraged. Thank you for sharing your life experiences and emotions openly and honestly. Your testimony is an encouragement to all who are struggling with addictions, searching for answers or feeling overwhelmed with the difficulties of life. It is a book that stimulates hope for the hopeless. We deeply appreciate your gifts of love!"

Chaplain Carole

"I want to tell you that I am so amazed by your book, I am really digesting it and thoughtfully answering all of the questions, it is ministering to me more than you can imagine!! I'm almost through the first section, but again thank you! Your book is speaking to me right where I am!"

Shelby

RECOVERY

# RECOVERY
## to
# DESTINY

### Journey to the Promised Land

By Deanna Allen

Daughters of Destiny
590 Hwy 105, Box 235
Monument, CO 80132-9125

http://www.ImpactLife.org/DaughtersofDestiny

ISBN: 978-0-9768438-7-0

Cover and Layout Design by CompounDesign, Copyright©2010
www.compoundesign.com

Developmental and copy editing by Lisa Abbott, freelance editor
lisaabbott@rocketmail.com

Printed in the United States of America

# Dedication

First, this book is dedicated to all Daughters of Destiny, their children and grand-children. My sisters whom I have cried with, laughed with, and shared the tough stuff with. For those who have found freedom even while being locked up–you have tasted the Promised Land. I have looked into your eyes and seen the pain of Egypt, the struggle of the Wilderness, and the hope of life in the Promised Land. I have watched an army of elite rise up and stand in the face of adversity and persecution, and yet triumph against all odds.

Micah 4:7 says,"I will transform the battered into a company of the elite. I will make a strong nation out of the long lost, a showcase exhibit of GOD's rule in action, as I rule from Mount Zion, from here to eternity."(MSG)

Next, this book is dedicated to every individual who has been, will be or is incarcerated. May it bring hope and help in your time of need. Please share it with your family, as we know that many of our struggles are generational. You can break the chain and stop the cycle. Let it end with you.

This book is also dedicated to every individual who is imprisoned but has never been arrested. You know who you are. You live in an emotional cell behind a fence of brokenness. We were designed to live victorious, glorious, abundant lives filled with peace, hope, and love. May you find these things on your journey to the Promised Land.

# Table of Contents

RECOVERY

# Foreword

Deanna Allen is passionate about life, faith, and ministry! Stepping into a room where she is speaking is like entering a highly charged atmosphere that is exploding with renewed hope, courageous faith, and compassionate intervention. This woman is a dynamic communicator of God's truth and *Recovery to Destiny* will give you a toolbox filled with resources that will positively change your life for the better.

Eric Liddell, the Olympian, once said: "Circumstances may appear to wreck our lives and God's plans, but God is not helpless among the ruins." In this book Deanna shares her shocking personal story of abuse, addiction, and personal choices that led to pain, destruction, and to the potential of destroying her own life. Deanna was walking around in what she powerfully describes as her own Egypt, a place of slavery and bondage that blinded her eyes to any possibility of "the promised land." But she, too, discovered that God does His best work when we are at the end of our rope. Her faith has made a profound difference in her thinking, her decisions, and in her journey to purposeful action as she inspires audiences all over the country with the truths in this book.

Deanna includes testimonials of people she has met who have wandered in their own kind of "wilderness" and their stories help her to demonstrate keys to lasting change and transformed living. She knows the power of unlocking the truth of God's Word and defeating the lies of the enemy by using the Sword of the Spirit. This book provides a map that will enable you to take steps toward truth and righteousness and it will help you to put a magnifying glass on your heart daily so your own choices will be based on God's Word.

My only child is incarcerated in a maximum security prison with a life without the possibility of parole sentence and I am grateful that Deanna dedicates a major part of her time to ministering to those who are living behind bars. As she shares her personal journey and the principles in this book, she is leading many out of the wilderness of self-doubt, wrong choices, and addictive patterns to the truth of Jesus Christ. She gives all of us the tools to challenge people to step into the destiny God has for their lives as they discover ultimate victory through His strength.

You'll want to purchase one book for your own reference library and ten more to give to people who need to know that they, too, can live with a new kind of freedom in an adventure of a lifetime as a Daughter or Son of Destiny!

Carol Kent
Speaker; Author, *When I Lay My Isaac Down* (NavPress),
*A New Kind of Normal* (Thomas Nelson)

# Acknowledgements

In life, many people make a mark or imprint in our heart and we are left changed forever. My life is a tapestry of hundreds, even thousands, of these faces and names. Of course, the person who has made an eternal difference is my Lord and Savior, Jesus Christ. Without His love, acceptance, forgiveness, and tenderness toward me, I would still be back in my garage, in the midst of my darkness and despair, spinning a life of destruction and pain. If you've seen Him – you've seen the Father.

The love of Jesus made me whole and allowed me to restore my relationship with the love of my life, Mitch. Your support and encouragement has helped me to soar over the past decade, and from that height, God has given me the words that have been spoken and written.

To my children, who have sacrificed time with mom and material comforts as we poured into the vineyard, endured days with dad, and kept our home in order–you truly are Team Allen. I am blessed beyond measure when I watch the gifts God has placed in each one of you. Andreia, Elizabeth, Christa, Joshua and Caleb, if God never asked another thing of me, raising you would be enough. You truly are an inheritance and great reward. My arrows being trained and prepared. I pray that the ceiling of our experiences in the things of God are but your floor.

Michelle, thanks for being a faithful right hand, ministry partner, and armor bearer. You have been well prepared for your calling and have become quite the trophy of grace. Shine for Jesus, sister! I could not have asked for a better confidante, companion, and friend.

To my dear sister PEZ, for opening up yourself and pouring out your stories during the writing of this book. For the many hours we shared crying, praying, and studying, while we fought for our own freedom so that we could live the message. Here is to the ministry of the moment. Planes, trains, and automobiles; there are many more adventures to be lived.

To the body of believers around the world who have truly become my adopted family; brothers and sisters in Christ. A body of water that doesn't move stagnates. Thanks for keeping me moving.

I couldn't release this book without acknowledging my parents. I want all the readers to know that my relationships with my mom and dad are flourishing today. I love both of my parents and consider them to be great people. I am a perfect blend of both of them and wouldn't be who I am were it not for them.

# Introduction
## Your Journey to the Promised Land

Times, fashion, and our surroundings may change, but the condition of the human heart has and always will remain the same. The Bible will never lose its relevance; because it addresses our nature and problems at a spiritual level. If you read the stories in the Bible; I guarantee you that you will find yourself in one of them. I see a parallel between modern-day addiction and recovery and the bondage and escape of the Israelites in the Old Testament.

Have you read the book of Exodus? It's a great story. The Israelites were God's chosen people, but millions of them were living as slaves in Egypt. If you are bound by an addiction of any kind, you are a slave to it; you are in bondage. You may even be addicted to a recovery program. The Israelites weren't experiencing God's greatest blessings for their lives. My guess is that if you are reading this book, you're not experiencing God's greatest blessings, either.

Through a series of miraculous events, God used a man named Moses to liberate the Israelites from slavery. After leaving Egypt, they walked for several years through the desert, until they came to a lush and beautiful land—a land "flowing with milk and honey." For us, "milk and honey" may represent peace, joy, freedom, prosperity, health, a good job, a nice home, a nice car, but most importantly, purpose! God wants to fill our lives with so much wisdom and provision that it overflows into the lives of people who are empty.

When the Israelites got to the Promised Land, they were frightened by the giants who lived there, even though their all-powerful God had assured them they could possess it. Throughout this book, you will read about miracles God performed to help the Israelites escape from Egypt and survive in the desert. At times, you may scratch your head in disbelief. You may wonder why they didn't trust God to conquer the giants. He demonstrated His power every time a problem arose, but they easily forgot when another problem popped up. Instead of saying, "God, you fixed the last problem and we know that You will fix this one too," they complained, grumbled, and doubted God.

Modern-day researchers figure the trip across the desert should have taken the Israelites only a matter of days. But because of their lack of faith and their disobedience to God, they wandered aimlessly for four decades. On our journey, we, too, will face giants. There will always be problems. How we act in the middle of the problem will determine how long we stay in it. God may either tell us to take another lap around the mountain or He may offer safe passage into the Promised Land, depending on our obedience, faith, and trust in Him. He hasn't changed!

It wasn't that the Israelites wanted to live in the desert rather than walk into God's promises. They wanted what God had to offer, but without doing what God said to get there. Sound familiar? They were used to their way of life. Some of them said they actually preferred slavery back in Egypt. God wanted to bless them, but He also wanted them to obey, trust, and love Him. He wants the same from us, too. God let His people wander around in the wilderness for forty years. What finally ended this vicious cycle? What did it take to cause a breakthrough? The answer is very simple; belief, faith, and trust in God. Only two men believed they could conquer the giants and possess The Promised Land. And guess what? They were the two who saw God's promise fulfilled. They believed and they received.

These two men weren't bigger or stronger than the average guy. They didn't have weapons of mass destruction. They didn't have machine guns or rocket launchers. They had something even better. They had a promise from God, and so do you! They knew that from a physical standpoint, their situation looked impossible, but that with God on their side, all things are possible. God wants you to know that, too!

After the first generation of Israelites died, the next generation victoriously took the land because they trusted God. They received wonderful blessings that their parents could have enjoyed many years earlier, if they had not doubted God.

This Bible story embodies the central theme of *Recovery to Destiny*. Each one of us fits into this Bible story somewhere. We are on a journey out of bondage into a glorious destiny.

So here's the big question:
Where are *you* in this journey? Here are the three options:

#1 – You are a slave in Egypt.

You are enslaved. You feel trapped, abandoned, broken, unworthy, insecure, unattractive, helpless or hopeless. But you are getting sick and tired of being sick and tired. A little voice in your head whispers that there must be more to life than this. There *is* more to life than this! Read on, my friend, and you will hear some incredible stories of people just like you who have broken the chains of hopelessness and bondage. They have escaped from slavery in Egypt and found new life and freedom in Christ. I thank God that you are sick of Egypt, because you will be amazed to discover your beautiful destiny in the Promised Land!

#2 – You are wandering in the Wilderness.

Maybe you've escaped from addiction and a deadly lifestyle and now you're going through recovery. Maybe you've been in recovery mode for a long time. Maybe you feel as if you're walking on a treadmill, covering the same old ground over and over again. Maybe you hear voices in your head calling you back to Egypt; back to your addiction. You didn't have to work so hard there. It's easier to look back, because you may wonder if you can ever make it to the Promised Land. Don't give up hope when you are almost there! You can move beyond recovery! Your wonderful destiny is closer than you think!

#3 – You are gloriously walking into your Promised Land; your destiny.

Praise God that the chains of Egypt have no power over you anymore. Praise God that your time in the Wilderness of recovery is over. Now you are jumping into your glorious destiny with both feet–freefalling into the hands of God–and there's no turning back! Incredible things await you in the Promised Land. Now is the time to watch our amazing Lord turn every bad thing you've ever experienced into a catalyst for helping others, and for bringing shame to the devil. Everything that the enemy planned for evil can now be used for good, and that's the miraculous wonder of walking into your destiny.

Identify which of these three categories you fit in. As you continue to read this book, you'll find encouragement in your journey and practical help to break the chains of Egypt and overcome the giants. A land flowing with milk and honey is just over the next hill!

In the coming pages, you'll hear more about Egyptians, Israelites, and their historic battles, but this is not just ancient history. This is YOUR story! This is your moment to rise above the darkness and shine like the stars! Are you ready to embark on the most exciting expedition of your life? Are you ready to walk out of slavery, through the Wilderness of recovery, into the Promised Land that God has prepared for you here and now? I sure hope so. I am so excited to take this journey with you into your glorious destiny.

# Deanna's Story
## My Escape from Egypt

*Here's the story of my escape from the Egypt that had become my own personal hell.* – Deanna

"Why won't you let me die?" I screamed. "Why?"

God and I were having a knock-down, drag-out fight. There He stood, calmly twirling the universe on His fingers, patiently watching and waiting, while I burned with rage in my cold, dark garage. I shook my fist at Him.

"Why do I have to live this life of hell? What kind of a God are You, anyway?"

I weighed a whopping 88 pounds, but I was not backing down from this encounter with the God of all creation. I grabbed my glass pipe and threw it violently to the floor, watching it shatter into a thousand pieces.

Just like my life, I thought.

I was out of control. I was beyond anger, fed up with the life I had been forced to live. I had experienced twenty-four years of suffering. My drugs couldn't help me anymore. My second daughter was dead and buried. I had just given birth to my third daughter from a third father. My kids were locked in the house, while I raged out in the garage, buried in my dark place of isolation.

This was my "meltdown moment;" my personal Hiroshima. I wasn't going anywhere until all the bombs had exploded and the damage had been done. I had twenty-four years of questions and I wasn't leaving this concrete bunker until they were answered.

It's a strange thing to desire death so desperately, but feel it is just out of reach. I first tried to take my life when I was twelve years old, but I failed. After that, I practiced what I call "suicide on the installment plan." Live life in the fast lane. Use all the drugs you can. Starve yourself to death. Gradually wither away to nothing. So far, it seemed to be working; except for the part where you go to sleep and never wake up again. I was mad at God for not cooperating. I was angry, tormented, and broken. All I wanted to do was die and meet my Maker with this one word on my lips:

"Why?"

Such a complicated little question. Why doesn't anyone care? Why doesn't anyone even notice? God, if You are so powerful and so loving; why do I have to live my life this way? "Where were You when I was beaten, used, abused, and abandoned? "Why did You just sit and watch me get raped and molested? What kind of a God are You? Is this a sick joke of Yours? I hope You're happy up there in Your heaven, because life sure sucks down here in hell. "Why can't I just die in peace? Why"

~~~~~

To understand the events that led up to that moment, you have to go back twenty-some years. Imagine a little princess named Deanna, who was raised in the *perfect* home. At least, that was the image. We had a nice big house in the middle of the California orchards. We were financially secure. My mom drove a big Cadillac. I went to the best schools. I always had a smile on my face; at least for the camera. At three years of age, I was thrown into a life of performance for approval, through my dancing and singing. For nearly ten years, I competed in pageants all over the country. It was grueling. I sat for hours getting my hair and makeup done. I practiced my routines endlessly, but it was never enough.

*"Smile, Deanna!"* That was a threat, not an encouragement.

"Go out there and kick their little butts." Winning was all that mattered.

 If I took second place instead of first; if I took "Little Miss Photogenic" instead of "Little Miss State," I faced mountains of disappointment, rejection, guilt, and shame. It was a heavy weight for one little girl to bear. After several years, I absolutely knew that love and acceptance were not free. They had to be earned. I thought that I didn't even deserve to be loved.

Performance became more than just a stage routine. It became a lifestyle. "Smile, Deanna. Don't forget your steps. Put on the charm. The world is watching, Deanna, so don't look bad. It will go against your marks. You're *nobody* if you're anything less than perfect."

I constantly lived with the choking pressure and fear of blowing it. And deep down inside, I knew that the best I had to offer would never be enough.

Meanwhile, our little town had nothing but good things to say about our family. My parents swam in and out of all the reputable circles. Even I believed the lie; that we were living the best of lives–that is, until our world fell apart. When I was eleven; my parents announced that they were getting a divorce. The Disneyland smiles and facades dissolved overnight. Mom and Dad spent millions of dollars in attorney fees. Their brutal divorce lasted longer than their marriage. The message they were sending my younger brother, E.J. and I was that their fight to destroy each other was more important to them than we were.

Just prior to the devastating announcement that our family was falling apart, my foster brother had molested me while my parents were away doing their own thing. He abused me in other ways, with the help of my foster sister and her friend. The irony is that everyone thought we were such a beautiful family for rescuing those poor, helpless children. The foster kids were always teenagers who had been bounced from home to home; kids no one else wanted. But who wanted *me*? Who would rescue *me*? I felt like the foster kids were more important than me and my brother. No wonder I became so angry.

I also was molested by my Girl Scout leader's husband. You might wonder where my parents were, and why they weren't protecting me. I asked myself that question a thousand times. While they were retreating further into their own little worlds, my sense of abandonment and rage grew. Money and prestige seemed more important to my mother than I was. My father's attention came in the form of shouting, beatings, and verbal abuse. Who needs that kind of attention? I knew I didn't.

I pulled further away from my parents, and drew closer to my brother, E.J., and my friends. We smoked and listened to music on our boom box down by the creek. We hung out with the break dancers and sported khaki pants, low-rider Chola shoes, and baby oil in our hair. Shoplifting also gave me a thrill, as did writing poetry, or starring in the school play. Now that was something I could do well. Just put me on stage and let me become somebody else in exchange for a little applause and affirmation. What a great way to escape from reality.

All those things came and went, but the drugs and alcohol stuck. I bragged that I could bury sixteen shots of tequila. I felt cool for being able to drink 200-pound high school football players under the table. You can probably guess how long that thrill lasted. But what else could I find to numb the pain?

When I was fifteen, my dad beat me for the last time. I don't remember what I had done wrong–usually it was nothing. Sometimes my little brother got me in trouble–like the time he put dish soap in the Jacuzzi and blamed it on me. This time it was the middle of the night. I was sound asleep when my dad came in, shouting. He started hitting me, screaming that he was going to kill me. I crawled out of bed in a daze. He chased me out of the house, yelling and hitting me all the way. Then he locked the doors. I banged on the front door and honked the car horn, but I could do nothing to get back inside.

I didn't know where to go or what to do. Imagine me; teen-aged girl in sleep-ware, stumbling through the pitch-black orchards and over irrigation pipes, bruised and beaten, muddy from head to toe, running past illegal immigrant workers' shacks. The tenant of our rental property threatened me with a shotgun in my face when I attempted to borrow a phone. I finally ended up spending the night with a high school coach, whom I barely knew. All the while, I was still stuck in the performance role. All I could think about was, "How am I going to protect our good family name?" I was prepared to continue living a family lie. After all, that's what we do! Isn't it? This thinking is very dysfunctional.

I thought that things would blow over by the next morning–that was how it usually went with my dad. Instead, everything went from bad to worse. He changed the locks on our house and told my brother a lie–that I was a whore living with a grown man. As it turned out, his words actually were prophetic. What were the options for an abandoned, 15-year-old girl who wanted to quietly finish high school with her friends in her hometown? I couldn't think of many. So, I prostituted myself to the high school coach in exchange for food, rent, and some extremely wild parties.

That bad relationship was followed by another, and another, and another. There were more beatings, drugs, alcohol, and dysfunction. I didn't know about healthy relationships. I couldn't be faithful to any man because I didn't trust men. I was the queen of sabotage. At the first sign that I might be hurt, *KA BOOM!* I'd blow that relationship apart. I had three babies by three different fathers. I had two abortions. I believed that I wasn't fit to bring any more children into the world. I endured the extremely traumatic death of my second daughter, who was born with a genetic defect. My anger, hostility, and rage grew more venomous–a generational curse I could have lived without. It was like a filthy disease and I knew of no cure.

~~~~~

Looking back at my "meltdown moment" in the garage, I saw myself as a two-year-old child, throwing a temper tantrum. All that pent-up emotion took me right back to where I started this crazy journey of life; back to a simple little girl with simple dreams of innocence. The little girl inside of me only wanted to know that somebody loved her; that somebody believed she was lovely and worth protecting; that she was cherished; that she was precious in somebody's eyes. She didn't want her value to be measured by her successes and failures.

So, when my rage melted and my "You owe me God!" words were all exhausted, I crumbled in tears to the floor. My anger left. Something like a sigh of relief came over me. Suddenly, I was a helpless little girl at the feet of a very big and compassionate God. I lay broken, on the floor, among the splinters of my glass pipe. I had little hope of ever getting my life back together. I had needed to reach that place of brokenness and surrender for many years.

Through the sobs; like a helpless little girl, I simply cried out to Jesus: "If you're not going to let me die, then please….please show me how to live. Please, God, won't You help me?"

At that moment, something miraculous happened within the stony walls of my heart. Incredibly, the hardness began to soften. Winter's curse remained, but I sensed a hint of springtime. For the first time, I saw a tiny crack of light shining into the dark, dark prison of my heart. I understood the futility of all my previous attempts to escape; that trying to numb the pain had all been a stupid waste of years. As I lay there, beside the broken glass shards and the pathetic legacy of my life, I knew what I must do. I had to begin again. I was ready to crawl toward freedom.

But God….I don't know the way.

I didn't know it at the time, but I had taken my very first step out of Egypt. God gave me a *new* heart with *new* desires. I finally understood that I was a slave, in bondage to my sin. God was the only one who could deliver me. In my weakness, I was asking Him to be my strength.

The Bible tells us that all hell broke loose when the Israelites decided to leave their slavery in Egypt. Pharaoh used every means possible to keep them enslaved. All kinds of gruesome obstacles stood in my path, too: financial nightmares, destructive relationships, drugs, bad attitudes and habits, and my distorted perception of God, myself and others.

Despite these obstacles, my faith grew as I went to church, read my Bible, and began to pray more seriously. God began to steer me toward better relationships and helped me to close the doors on bad ones. He taught me that I didn't have to live with boyfriends or manipulate people to survive. I was a baby in my relationship with God. I cried out to Him like never before. As I did, He surrounded me physically, mentally, emotionally, and spiritually. His thumbprint was on my life daily, and it was a very cool time. Scary, but cool.

My most difficult battle was my drug addiction. I had tried many times to quit, and every time, I failed. I looked into detox programs and residential treatment homes. My greatest fear was that if I checked myself into a residential treatment center, the fathers of my two children could prove I was an unfit mother, and the courts could take my kids from me. It was a huge obstacle, but I reluctantly delivered my kids to their fathers and took the plunge into a residential program.

My recovery didn't happen overnight. Little by little, God took me away from the bondage of my addiction–my Egypt–through the Wilderness; closer and closer to the Promised Land. All the while, I knew that with just one bad decision, I'd throw it all away and find myself back in slavery. I attended many recovery meetings, support groups and read a lot of books. I knew all the recovery steps and all the clever sayings, inside and out.

The best advice I received came from a friend at church, who said, "You're taking all these steps to get better. Why don't you take the one step that will change your life forever? Step completely to Jesus. He is your strength. He's the answer you're looking for."

This idea sounded good to me. It also sounded too simple, but I knew my friend was right. I committed my life to God completely, holding absolutely nothing back from Him. I learned to rely on His strength in my weakness. I had simple conversations with Him about everything: "God, I don't feel very good today! God, I don't think I can do this!"

I found there is no magic formula to developing a relationship with Jesus Christ. Often, it happens through simple, heartfelt conversations, and by reading His word.

I learned to cling to my Heavenly Father like never before. I experienced unconditional love for the first time. I stopped running from my past. I stopped trying to earn people's approval by putting on a good performance. And for the first time ever, I saw myself as a beautiful little girl, with all of my innocence restored–a little girl who was loved and cherished by her proud Papa.

*And he said, I tell you the truth, unless you change and become like little children, you will never enter the kingdom of heaven.* (Matthew 18:3, NIV)

If you allow that scripture to penetrate your heart, it will truly set you free! Just as children depend on their parents, God wants us to depend on Him. He wants us to come to Him with a teachable spirit. He wants us to shed off what the world has taught us. He wants us to start all over with Him. When Jesus speaks of the kingdom of heaven, He isn't talking about a place where we go when we die. He is talking about the kingdom of heaven right here on earth—The Promised Land! The place where we experience an abundant life here and now; where we find freedom from our past, forgiveness, hope, peace, joy, unconditional love, acceptance, and provision.

To this day, I feel like a little girl when I am in His presence; and being loved by Him is all that really matters to me.

~~~~~

My life is a testimony of God's power and ability to reach into the gutter and make something precious out of a crumbled, dirty piece of rubbish. I'm a walking miracle because of what God has done! He receives all the glory. At one point in my life, I was a hopeless dope fiend. Today, I'm a dopeless hope fiend!

So what is *your* story? Wherever you are in this journey, I believe you'll find a lot of hope and encouragement in the pages ahead. Did you know that your story can have a beautiful ending? Do you believe that's possible? I do, because if God can transform a life that was as hopeless as mine, He can do the same for you.

As we launch into this sometimes painful, but wonderful healing journey, I pray that your heart will be opened wide. I pray that God will help you understand why this book is in your hands. I don't believe it is by "coincidence." I pray that you will find total freedom; that whatever chains are holding you back, they will fall like dust to the ground. I pray that you will be radically transformed. And I thank God for the opportunity to spend this time with you.

Enjoy the adventure! And let me know what treasures you find along the way. My address is in the back of the book in the contact me section so you can share your journey with me. When you finish, I think you'll agree with me (and God) that *you* are a treasure! That's exactly how your Father sees you. You are precious!

Now let's put on our walking shoes….and don't forget your backpack! They'll be helpful along the way. Learn how to use the items inside and you will get farther faster.

# Our Backpack
## Tools for the Journey! !

This journey is only possible if you have the right tools for the job:

**A Key** to open doors, unlock the chains that bind us, and open the treasure chest of incredible things God wants to give us. For example, forgiveness is a key to help us trust others; truth is a key to free us from lies; accountability is a key to encourage us.

**A Pair of Shoes** to help you run the race before you, so you can finish with strength and courage.

**A Butterfly** to remind you that the Lord wants to take you out of your cocoon and transform you into a beautiful new creation.

**A Map** to lead you out of Egypt and guide you to the Promised Land. You will need God's direction for every choice you'll make.

**Prayer** to communicate with your God and Father.

**A Sword** to fight the lies Satan will tell you along the way. The Bible says that the truth of God's Word is like a two-edged sword.

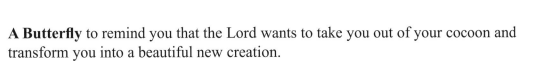

**A Magnifying Glass** to honestly examine your ways and test their truth and purity.

**A Ruler** to measure your growth and to see how far you've come.

**A Pencil** to capture ideas, journal, and answer questions.

**A Stone** to remind us not to judge others who may be at different points in their own journey to the Promised Land of recovery.

**Scissors** to cut out anger, gossip, grumbling, or complaining. These old habits will slow down your progress.

**Eye Glasses** to see things more clearly. God changes our perspective and allows us to see His spiritual kingdom of light and life.

Grab your backpack and let's get going! Let's start by taking off our worldly glasses. Let's put on God's eyeglasses so we can see Egypt clearly. Let's take a good look at the things that enslave us and kill our souls, so that we won't ever be tempted to think that Egypt was better than life on the road to the Promised Land.

# In Egypt–"Wish You Were Here!"
## Part 1

Hey, friend!

Everything is just great here in Egypt.
I'm having so much fun with all these
beautiful, happy people. I'm glad I came.
Wish you were here to share the
excitement. It's awesome! Give my love
to all.

Happy-go-Lucky

P.S. Here are a few
snapshots of Egypt. Sorry,
without our fancy computers
we can't touch up these
snapshots, so you'll have to
see the untouched pictures.
Enjoy them!

## Snapshots of Egypt

Hi, I'm Deanna.

Of the many snapshots of my slavery in Egypt, here's one that stands out in my mind: I was pregnant with my boyfriend's baby. It was our one-year anniversary. I wanted to do something special with him, but he wanted to go out and party with his friends. We got into a fight that became real nasty. As he got up in my face, I was thinking, If you touch me I'm going to kill you. You take me out, or I'll take you out!

I obviously had lost my mind, because he was a professional boxer. He cocked his arm back and held his fist aimed at my face with a look that said, If you don't back off, you will get hit!

I was so angry! I said, "You might as well hit me now!" So he did. He hit me right on the jaw and I heard the bone crack.

I wasn't as tough as I thought I was. I felt a fire rip through my jaw. The fact that I could barely speak didn't even stop me. The anger and adrenaline made me absolutely crazy. "You blew it!" I said. "You should have knocked me out!" I then kicked him in the jaw and his top teeth penetrated my foot.

He chased me into the house and pushed me. I grabbed a knife off the counter and threatened to kill him. As we stood there, face to face, my heart was racing. It felt as though time stood still. I finally asked him to leave. I am thankful that he did, or one of us probably wouldn't have walked away alive. And that's how we celebrated our first anniversary. Can you say drama?

Hi, I'm E.J.

(As remembered by Deanna. E.J. is my little brother.)

Egypt for E.J. was a place of rage, anger, and pure insanity. He was like a jar of nitroglycerin; the slightest disturbance and ka-boom! You wouldn't even know what set him off! Out of nowhere he yelled, screamed, and punched doors. He banged his head against walls. He took bills out of his wallet and ripped them to shreds. He called the people that loved him vile and vicious names. One day, he threatened to burn down my house with my children inside.

Another time, he got into it with his girlfriend at her mom's house. He literally was like the Tasmanian devil. He tore down everything in his path. He stomped up and down the stairs. He smashed and kicked things. He stood outside of her house and shouted vile obscenities. His girlfriend had finally had enough of her mom's house being destroyed, so she took off in the car, but not soon enough. E.J. opened the car door and jumped in while she was driving away. He grabbed the steering wheel and started to swerve all over the road.

She finally stopped the car, got out, and started walking. E.J. had managed to cool down enough to start sweet talking to her. (So she thought.) "Come on baby. Get in the car. Let's talk," he urged.

He finally persuaded her to get back in the car and he drove away. He then jumped on the freeway and started yelling at her again. It was only by the grace of God that she was able to get him to stop the car and let her out again. She called the police and E.J. was arrested for stealing her mom's car. That was just one day in E.J.'s life, but it seemed like almost every day was full of drama. His rage constantly got him into trouble.

*Hi, I'm Cris.*

*As I look back over my experiences in Egypt, it's a wonder I even made it out of that place alive. I was a walking contradiction. I played the role of a good girl on the outside, while I was dying on the inside. I looked for ways to take others with me. I wore a smile to cover my dying soul. I chose which mask to wear for the day, depending on whom, what, and where I would be.*

*My emotions came from my childhood abuse. They were reinforced by my bad choices and how people treated me. My life was a bottomless pool of poison and pain. I tried to cover up the pain and pretend it wasn't there. I became a performer and learned to disappear into the act.*

*When I was sixteen, I ventured into self-mutilation. I crashed my fist into a wooden pallet. As my flesh ripped, it caused an instant release of pain and pent-up emotion. I felt a false sense of control and relief. I did it over and over again. That release became harder and harder to find; even as my behavior took on different forms and became more self-destructive. I became numb to the physical pain I was causing to my own body.*

*That ugly monster of self-injury controlled me for most of my life. But publicly, I kept on my happy face. I also used prescription drugs to cope with my pain. At my worst I was taking up to 120 pills a day. At that point, I was the mother of three children and married to a man who was becoming a pastor. Ironically, I was leading women's, children's, and youth ministries. I also worked as an administrator for a Christian school, forming policies to protect others from people just like me.*

*The thief [Satan] comes only to steal, kill, and destroy. I [Jesus] have come so that you might have life – life in all its fullness.* (John 10:10)

In many ways, we humans are like cute little lambs being lured into a den of wolves. We go out searching for fun, good times, friendship, and love. And what do we find? We find death. That's what happened in the three snapshots above. They are all true stories. Each of the paths led to death! While some choices lead to physical death, many more choices lead people to death in relationships, value of self, hope, or joy. Sin kills the good in our life, leaving our life looking like a wasteland.

So, what do we mean by "Egypt?"

Egypt represents living your life apart from God and following the lies of Satan. It's a painful life of sin and temptation that leads to destruction and eternal hell. The Israelites were slaves in Egypt and so are we. Satan enslaves us with addictions, abuse, gambling, food, money, smoking, work, spending, relationships, sex, drugs, alcohol, cussing, gossiping, provocative dancing, prostitution, and more. We build our own prisons of unforgiveness and anger.

*Why are we living in Egypt?*

*What do we really want to get out of life?*

*What's the point of our high school games?*

*We spin out of control, looking for love and acceptance.*

*But would we even know love if we found it?*

*Where does it all lead?*

*Why don't we get out of here?*

In the Bible, Jesus actually compares us to sheep. In case you didn't know it, sheep are not very smart. *One* thing about sheep, however, is amazing. They know their master's voice. They will not respond to the voice of a stranger!

Jesus said, *"My sheep listen to my voice; I know them, and they follow me."* (John 10:27, NIV)

A good shepherd tends to his flock with compassion and a watchful eye. When a lamb strays from the flock, it often becomes tangled and lost. Then along comes the good shepherd. He searches out the lamb and untangles it. After he rescues the wayward lamb from the mess it's in, he lifts it up and places it across his big, strong shoulders, and carries it back to safety.

In a nutshell, your relationship with Jesus Christ will look like a lot like the relationship between the sheep and their shepherd. Until you experience Him for yourself, you cannot fathom the depths of His love, power, and protection!

None of us sets out looking for death. We seek happiness. But as long as we search in Egypt, we will find death. One of the most awesome, powerful benefits of living in the Promised Land is the ability to recognize the voice of the Almighty God–the Good Shepherd!

I'll say it again: *All paths in Egypt lead to death.*

Satan has dominion over Egypt. As long as you live there, you will follow his cunning, deceptive voice. His sole purpose is to keep you living outside of God's promise. He dangles tasty lies in front of our faces: exciting parties, sex, lots of money, incredible highs, all the thrills of living fast and free. But those temptations are about as real as a Hollywood movie set. Sure, they may taste sweet for a few days, weeks, or even a few years. But they will always, *always* poison us in the end. Remember that "The thief comes only to steal, kill, and destroy." (John 10:10) Every one of Satan's tantalizing temptations leads to death.

*There is a way that seems right to a person, but eventually it ends in death. (Proverbs 14:12)*

*Even Satan can disguise himself to look like an angel of light. (2 Corinthians 11:14)*

Thankfully, one path leads to life. Jesus said, *"I am the way, the truth, and the life."* (John 14:6, NIV)

He is the only One who gives us "life in all its fullness" (Colossians 2:10 MSG)

Are you ready to learn more about that path to life? It's the only way to leave the death-clouded land of Egypt behind and come into the glorious destiny that God has prepared for you. Don't forget your tools.

# Being in Bondage
## Part 1.1

Remember the story of the Israelites who were enslaved in Egypt? You may wonder how they ended up in Egypt in the first place. It wasn't their home. The Bible tells us that they traveled to Egypt during a seven-year famine, because a man named Joseph was in charge of all the Egyptian grain. Joseph told his father that he would care for their family in Egypt. Somehow, their seven-year visit ended up lasting 400 years. During that time, that one family increased to over a million people. Here's what happened next:

*A new king came to power in Egypt who didn't know Joseph. He spoke to his people in alarm, "There are way too many of these Israelites for us to handle. We've got to do something: Let's devise a plan to contain them, lest if there's a war they should join our enemies, or just walk off and leave us."*

*So they organized them into work-gangs and put them to hard labor under gang-foremen. They built the storage cities Pithom and Ramses for Pharaoh. But the harder the Egyptians worked them the more children the Israelites had--children everywhere! The Egyptians got so they couldn't stand the Israelites and treated them worse than ever, crushing them with slave labor. They made them miserable with hard labor--making bricks and mortar and back-breaking work in the fields. They piled on the work, crushing them under the cruel workload. (Exodus 1:8-14, MSG)*

What a comparison to those of us who have fallen into addiction and bondage. Our enemy may not be the Egyptian king. But like Pharaoh, our enemy, Satan, sees that there are too many people walking toward God. He's afraid that we'll find our way out of his camp and begin living out the destiny that God has planned for us. So he devised a plan with his sub-rulers (his demons) to enslave us and keep us in chains. He introduces things into our lives that keep us trapped in the darkness, with no hope of freedom, or of ever seeing the light. His primary goal is to keep us deceived

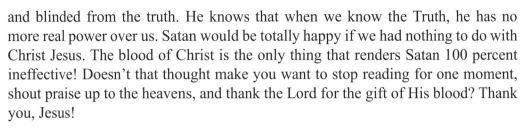

and blinded from the truth. He knows that when we know the Truth, he has no more real power over us. Satan would be totally happy if we had nothing to do with Christ Jesus. The blood of Christ is the only thing that renders Satan 100 percent ineffective! Doesn't that thought make you want to stop reading for one moment, shout praise up to the heavens, and thank the Lord for the gift of His blood? Thank you, Jesus!

Sometimes, Satan uses subtle tactics to keep us in bondage. I once visited the country of Egypt with my husband, Mitch. As we walked the streets of Cairo, we were astonished by the amount of dust, exhaust, and pollution. It's an overcrowded and under-regulated city, so to us, it felt very chaotic and unhealthy. But for the people who lived there, it was normal. They did not see the brown, smoggy sky as a problem. Similarly, for those of us who are spiritually and morally bankrupt, life can be slowly killing us, but we don't even know it. While you're in Egypt, you don't even realize that anything is wrong. It's just "normal" life. When Jesus rescues us, it's like being taken out of fog and pollution. The sky suddenly looks so blue, the grass so green, the air is so fresh, everything is beautiful, and this heavy burden is lifted off of our hearts. God has such a great destiny planned for us!

Satan controls us with fear, but he's also afraid himself. Why? Because a spiritual battle is raging and he knows that he eventually will lose. According to the Bible, this world as we know it will come to an end some day and Satan's destiny is eternal punishment in a lake of fire. But for now, he is afraid that we'll join the side of his enemy–God! He is afraid we might actually walk off and leave him … that we might be delivered and set free.

*Keep your mind clear, and be alert. Your opponent the devil is prowling around like a roaring lion as he looks for someone to devour. (*1 Peter 5:8, *God's Word)*

Satan brings temptations into our lives that cause us to labor aimlessly and toil long hours with no fruit to show for our effort. Even though we serve his purposes, he still hates us and treats us worse and worse. He hopes that one day he might destroy us and our children forever. He crushes our spirits. He leads us to destroy our lives and the lives of others. In the verse from Exodus 1, did you notice how the Israelites were forced to make bricks? Satan uses that same trick today. He encourages us to build massive walls around ourselves and between each other. So many people die feeling completely hopeless that they can ever find a way out of their self-made prison. We break our own backs building this ruined mess that we call a life. I know I did!

I've already told you some of my own stories, so you can imagine the sickening amount of time and energy I wasted on unhealthy, toxic relationships. I wish I could recover all the time, money, and effort I spent staying high for a decade. I wish I could hold the babies I murdered through abortion. Toward the end of my time in Egypt, my life was a twisted pile of shrapnel. It felt as if my army had turned its weapons and bombed *me!* How much sense does that make!? But that's exactly what we do. We continue on with our self-destructive patterns until we are crushed under the cruel burden that we have heaped upon ourselves. The slave master cracks the whip and we obey until we can labor no more. We crumble to the ground, defeated and broken.

Since the time I left Egypt, God's piercing light has revealed many areas of dark denial in my life over the years. He showed me that I was at one time a prostitute – not like some women, who stand on street corners and take money for sexual favors. No, I was too sophisticated for that. But God showed me that using my sexuality, femininity, and manipulative powers to get what I wanted from men was a form of prostitution. I used my body and beauty to get into relationships with men who had access to drugs or things that I wanted. Thus, I was living as a prostitute. This is an example of the enemy's deception while we're living in Egypt.

Here's one more idea from the book of Exodus:

*These are the names of the sons of Israel (that is, Jacob) who came with him to Egypt with their families: Reuben, Simeon, Levi.* (Exodus 1:1)

Jacob (the father of Joseph, who was mentioned earlier) brought all his children into Egypt with him. Today, generational patterns of slavery cause parents to take their children and grandchildren into dark places of bondage and oppression. Some of us began life in slavery, not by our own choice. However, staying there *is* our own choice. God calls it our free will. He doesn't want to control our choices. He wants us to make choices based on a relationship of love and respect for Him; not because He forces us to.

## Stop And Think!

Some things from your own life may have come to mind as you've read this chapter. They may cause you to feel uncomfortable; maybe even guilty and shameful. It's okay to admit that you are living in Egypt. The first step toward freedom is to be honest about your condition. Someone once said that admitting you have a problem is half the cure. Let's rephrase that just a little: confessing your problems to God is half the cure. Invite Him in! He is a patient, precious gentleman and He is waiting for you. Jesus says, "Behold, I stand at the door and knock. If anyone hears My voice and opens the door, I will come in to him and will dine with him and he with Me." (Revelation 3:20, NKJV)

You need to look closely at the chains holding you back, before you can hope to be free of them. Otherwise, you might begin walking toward the Promised Land still feeling those chains pulling you back to Egypt. You can't move forward if you are always looking back. To illustrate this principle, try this right now: Walk across the room while trying to look backwards. Do you bump into things, stumble, or walk in a very crooked path?

Now, will you take a good honest look at your life? Is a heavy burden weighing you down? Can you clearly identify it? Is an addiction or a sinful lifestyle wearing you out? Are you allowing unforgiveness to isolate you?

Jesus said, *"Come to me, all you who are weary and burdened, and I will give you rest. Take my yoke upon you and learn from me, for I am gentle and humble in heart, and you will find rest for your souls. For my yoke is easy and my burden is light." (*Matthew 11:29-30, NIV*)*

List the habits, relationships, or situations that enslave you today:

_____

_____

_____

_____

_____

List any unresolved issues that have contributed to the slavery in your life, such as abuse or abandonment:

_____

_____

_____

_____

_____

Describe a time in your life (if any) where you felt as if you were walking toward God:

_____

_____

_____

_____

_____

Describe a time in your life when you felt the enemy working his hardest against you:

_____

_____

_____

_____

_____

These questions are not intended to bring more shame, but rather to help you confront your strongholds so that you can be released from them. The Bible says, "There is therefore now no condemnation to those who are in Christ Jesus, who walk not according to the flesh but according to the Spirit." (Romans 8:1, NKJV) Facing your issues straight on, with courage and faith, is the only way to be set free and become all that you were created to be. And there is no better time than the present to be FREE–truly free! The first step toward freedom is to confess everything to God through prayer and ask Him to help you.

*Cast your cares on the LORD and he will sustain you; he will never let the righteous fall. (*Psalms 55:22, *NIV)*

If you choose to cast your cares on the Lord, what do you have to lose?

_____

_____

_____

_____

_____

What do you have to gain?

_____

_____

_____

_____

What are you afraid of?

_____

_____

_____

_____

## PRAYER POINT

Father God, in the matchless name of Jesus, I pray that You would bring me comfort and counsel through Your Holy Spirit. Show me the things that are preventing me from walking in a pure and absolute relationship with You. I want to know You more, God. I want what You want for my life. Help me, God, to see my life as You see it. Help me to believe that my life won't always look like it does right now. Help me to walk by faith and not by sight. Help me to be still and know that You are God. Help me, Father, to receive Your love and acceptance.

Help me to surrender all the heavy burdens of my life to You and lay them at the foot of the cross….they are covered by Jesus' blood. I cannot carry this load any more. I need Your help in this journey, Lord. Show me the path that I should walk and point out the right roads for me to travel. Guide me by Your truth and teach me, for You are the God who saves. Save me Lord, from this mess I call my life. Restore in me a clean heart, God. Renew a steadfast spirit within me. Give me hope for the future and grace to travel this journey.

In Jesus' name. Amen.

Now, are you ready to take a few more steps toward deliverance? Great! Then let's move on, shall we?

RECOVERY

# The Lies of Slavery
## Part 1.2

**In My Addiction by Deanna Allen**
When I was in my addiction,
I felt like I was all alone;
I didn't know how I could stop,
Because of the rate at which it had grown.

This monster was larger than everything,
I was a slave to it indeed;
The things that used to matter,
Became so much less of a need.

My addiction had no heart,
And I've since seen many of its kind.
My addiction was a thief,
It nearly robbed me of my mind.

But my Redeemer had a better plan,
A greater purpose for my life;
His will was that I serve Him only,
Be a godly woman, mother, daughter, wife.

Now my addictions have no hold on me,
And I know He'll free you, too;
Just ask the Lord to be your strength,
Pray without ceasing,
And acknowledge Him in all you do.

*The weapons we use in our fight are not made by humans. Rather, they are powerful weapons from God. With them we destroy people's defenses, that is, their arguments and all their intellectual arrogance that oppose the knowledge of God. We take every thought captive so that it is obedient to Christ.* (2 Corinthians 10:4-5)

I've never heard of a child who dreams about becoming a prostitute, pimp, dealer or convict when she grows up. We don't set out to be enslaved by drugs or sexual addictions. No little boy aspires to spend his life standing before judges and going to prison. No little girl dreams of being beaten and raped in a string of abusive, dysfunctional relationships. These are not our dreams and aspirations in life. Nobody wants to be a slave in Egypt. Deep down, we all want to live quiet, happy lives.

Then why do we find ourselves trapped in slavery without any apparent hope of escape?

Because we have listened to the lies. We have been enticed by Satan's seductive voice and we willingly remain in his prison. But this was never God's intention for us.

*The devil was a murderer from the beginning. He has never been truthful. He doesn't know what the truth is. Whenever he tells a lie, he's doing what comes naturally to him. He's a liar and the father of lies.* (John 8:44)

*You will know the truth, and the truth will set you free.* (John 8:32)

The truth sets us free. The lies take away our freedom and imprison us. So, we have this constant tension between truth and lies; between God's voice and the voice of the devil, who is the "father of lies."

One of the strongest chains that enslaved me was the chain of dysfunctional relationships. The iron links of that chain were one bad relationship after another. Yes, I was a slave to the relationships, but; I also was a slave to the *lies that I believed about myself.* I had heard these lies all my life–lies that said, "You'll never be good enough. You're worthless. You're stupid. Nobody can love you." These lies led me from one dysfunctional relationship to another.

I could never earn the love and affection that I so desperately wanted. So, I became an extreme perfectionist, trapped in an excruciating performance cycle. And yet, I knew that my greatest accomplishments were worthless. Therefore *I thought I* was worthless. A mountain of guilt and shame rose like a heap of rotten filth over this little girl's innocent hopes and dreams. With all of that garbage mounting up, what type of people do you think I attracted and tolerated in my life? "Prince Charming" and "Princess Chastity" are not the right answers!

Maybe you can relate to my story. It's common for people who come from abusive relationships to be driven by performance and perfectionism. But it's also common for people to go in the opposite direction – to give up trying all together. That's what my brother E.J. did. He heard the same lies I did. But while I was killing myself trying to prove to the world that I was worth something, E.J. simply checked out and stopped trying. He basically said, "Why bother? Nobody cares about me. They think I'm trash and that I'll never amount to anything, so why should I disappoint them? It doesn't matter if people hate me or if I get in trouble with the law. It's better than trying to achieve an unreasonable standard that someone has set for my life. I won't even try."

## Worthless Lies

Both E.J. and I chose to accept the lies of Satan. We not only accepted them, but we actually built big shrines to validate them. It all began with those words we heard when we were little: "You are worthless." We believed the lie. Then we lived it.

*For as a man thinks in his heart, so is he.* (Proverbs 23:7)

This Bible verse talks about a self-fulfilling curse. If I believe I am worthless, then I am going to live like a worthless thing. I'm going to allow people to treat me like dirt. I am not going to pursue anything above what I think I deserve. And since I think I deserve nothing, I will settle for nothing. I will surround myself with nobodies. I don't deserve anything better. Can you see how we become slaves to this way of thinking?

Meanwhile, there's this conflict in our soul, because something inside of us is crying out that we *are* worth something. We *do* want to be noticed and affirmed. That voice is an echo of the *truth* in our spirits. And that voice comes from God.

You *are* worth something. In fact, you are priceless in God's eyes. He loves you with an eternal love. So don't believe the lies! Many brothers and sisters in Christ would find joy in showing you God's love and welcoming you into His family. You'll want and need people like this to encourage you in your journey to the Promised Land.

You are precious in God's eyes! The question is, whose voice will you listen to? The father of lies or the One who loves you and Whose Truth will set you free?

## Stop And Think!

What are some of the lies you were told or shown as a child or as a young adult?

_____

_____

_____

_____

_____

How have those lies shaped your life?

_____

_____

_____

_____

What situations have seemed to prove those lies to be true?

_____

_____

_____

_____

How do you define real truth?

_____

_____

_____

_____

_____

In what areas have you tried to earn the acceptance of others?

_____

_____

_____

_____

_____

How have you sought validation through people, experiences, or things?

_____

_____

_____

_____

_____

STOP & THINK

Can you relate to any of our stories?  If so, how?

_____

_____

_____

_____

_____

## Prayer Point

Jesus, You say in your Word that Your sheep will know Your voice. I want to be one of Your sheep. Up to this point, I have been Your enemy's puppet. I am being restrained by invisible strings. Please send Your Spirit of Truth to clear my confusion. I want my will to line up with Your will, but my will is being held captive. I want to believe that all things are possible with You. Lord, please rescue me. Open my eyes so I might have a more truthful perspective for my life. I am so tired of believing the lies and I desperately need the Truth. Jesus, You are the Truth. Through You, I am brought out of the kingdom of darkness into glorious light. Help me to come out of the lies right now.  Amen.

# Who's in Charge Here?
## Part 1.3

You might believe that you don't have any choices left. Or you might be scared to death of making the wrong choice. No one chooses to be molested, beaten or abandoned. It's not easy to realize that we have a choice whether or not to keep those chains on. Do you know that you have a choice?

Maybe you can relate to the stories in the previous chapter. Maybe you're like E.J., believing you are entitled to trash every person, place, and thing that crosses your path because of the way you've been treated. E.J. believed that his problems were always his mother or father's fault, or because of their divorce. It was never his fault. It's easier to blame other people for our mistakes because we think it takes the responsibility off of us. But we are just deceiving ourselves. *You* are responsible for you!

Your problems are *not* the problem. What's most important is *how you respond to your problems*. You don't choose to have bad things happen to you, but you *do* choose how to respond. Will you become bitter and imprisoned? Or can you allow God to take those awful things and turn them into something good; something for His glory, rather than for your destruction? Can you move on? Can you let go of those dysfunctional relationships and find healing? Can you forgive the people who have hurt you? Jesus showed us how to forgive. On the cross, He prayed for His murderers: "Father forgive them because they don't know what they are doing." (Luke 23:34)Wow! And He can help us love our enemies, as well. He loves us even when we are His enemy, and He wants us to do the same for each other.

Maybe you didn't choose to be a slave in Egypt. But the choice is yours whether or not to remain there. What will your choice be?

You can choose to leave today.

The choice is yours.

Who's in charge?

*Choose this day whom you will serve. As for me and my house, we will serve the Lord.* (Joshua 24:15)

Who will *you* serve? Or to put it another way: Who's in charge of your life? This is a critical question. We might feel helpless and powerless over many of our circumstances, but the truth is that we do have a choice. Oh yes, we do! Hopefully, this fact brings you a sense of freedom. You can choose to leave Egypt and enter the Promised Land under the powerful authority and loving direction of Jesus Christ.

You might get a little frustrated, perhaps even angry, about choosing who is in charge of your life. That choice places the burden of responsibility on you. But with the responsibility comes freedom. When you teach a child to tie his own shoes you give him a new responsibility, but you also offer him freedom. Think about that. Don't run away from making the choice about who is in charge of your life. You *can* throw off Satan's lies, although it won't always be easy. In fact, none of us is strong enough to do it alone. But God is strong enough, and He is simply waiting for us to surrender our lives to Him, to place our trust in Him. He will free us from slavery in Egypt, but only if we ask Him. So we need to decide if God gets control of our lives….or the devil. There is no middle ground.

*You cannot be a slave of two masters; you will hate one and love the other; you will be loyal to one and despise the other.* (Matthew 6:24)

*They still carry on their old customs to this day. They do not worship the Lord nor do they obey His laws and commands ... So those people worshiped the Lord, but they also worshiped their idols; and to this day their descendants continue to do the same.* (2 Kings 17:34,41)

## You Choose, But You Don't Control

If you think that you are in control, then you have believed the lies. Satan tries to make you think you can fix things and control your own destiny. This is a well traveled, dead-end that will leave you frustrated, exhausted, and disgusted. We are not strong enough to free ourselves from slavery, we have to be delivered—rescued! Until God rescues us, we are merely one of Satan's puppets.

This is a difficult concept to grasp, but it's so very important to understand: You choose, but you do not control.

You can choose to be freed from slavery, but you don't control your own destiny. You choose to give control of your life to Jesus and then He will change what you cannot.

There are plenty of alternatives to giving control of your life to Christ. You could give control to your boss or your job, hoping to find lasting fulfillment there. You could give your life to your children, hoping that they will give you warm, fuzzy feelings and a sense of eternal worth. You could enslave yourself to money and material possessions, building up an earthly kingdom that doesn't last. (See Matthew 6:20.)

Any pursuit other than Jesus has that potential. The job that fulfilled us and pumped up our self-esteem suddenly can be taken away. The thing that gave us a thrill or made us high begins to kill us. The once full bank account is now in the red. The child who was once so charming has become a pain in the assets. The lover who used to make our heart pound is now breaking it! Life on this planet sometimes seems like one big letdown after another.

If you confess that you are unable to get yourself out of the mess you've made, then there is hope! You are a lot closer to freedom than you think, because you are in a place where you can turn your will and your life over to someone who can truly help you.

There's only one source for the hope, contentment, and stability you need. Unfortunately, everything that this world offers will eventually let you down. No earthly thing brings lasting contentment or fulfillment. But don't lose hope! God will never leave you. He is continually working things together for a better future for you. He is the only One who can fix a broken person. He made you and He loves you. He can put you back together, but first, He wants you to willingly submit your life to Him.

What does it mean, to submit your life to God? Do you have to begin to live a perfect, spotless, unblemished life? No way! Do you suddenly become some faith-filled, super Christian? Well, that would be fantastic, but God isn't looking for a good performance. He isn't a judge whose love is conditional, based on how you are doing that day. No, He simply loves you because you are His child – not because of what you have done. His love for you will never change. He simply offers you freedom, hope, and fulfillment. But it still comes back to that one difficult decision: "Choose this day whom you will serve." The choice is yours.

Will you choose to give Jesus control of your life?

## The Choice is Yours

Maybe you didn't choose to be a slave in Egypt. But do you choose to remain there? Do you yearn to live somewhere else? Do you believe that God has a much better destiny for you? This destiny is so indescribably delicious that once you taste it, you will wonder why you ever waited so long to experience it.

*However, as it is written: "No eye has seen, no ear has heard, no mind has conceived what God has prepared for those who love him." (*1 Corinthians 2:9, *NIV*)

*Keep your mind on things above, not on worldly things. (*Colossians 3:2*)*

*Our lives are guided by faith, not by sight. (*2 Corinthians 5:7*)*

Keep your mind on the things of God and His promises. Believe what He says is true! Keep walking by faith toward what you know to be true, despite your circumstances. Be patient in the process. It takes some of us decades to mess our lives up this much, and yet we want them fixed overnight.

We may feel as if God has disconnected Himself at times, but that is not true.

*I will never abandon you or leave you. (*Hebrews 13:5*)*

That sounds like stability to me! If you are looking for**:**

Someone who will stay with you no matter what;

Someone who will not judge you;

Someone who can love you like no one else;

Someone who will never lie to you;

Someone who will never cheat you or steal from you;

Someone who knows how much you are worth,

Then give God a shot. Choose to let Him take charge of your life. He is the only One qualified to do it, and He will do a *great* job. Promise! It's all part of growing up and becoming a mature person in God's loving family; His Kingdom on earth!

*Until we become mature, until we measure up to Christ, who is the standard. Then we will no longer be little children, tossed and carried about by all kinds of teachings that change like the wind. We will no longer be influenced by people who use cunning and clever strategies to lead us astray. Instead, as we lovingly speak the truth, we will grow up completely in our relationship to Christ, who is the head.* (Ephesians 4:13-15)

Will this decision require some changes? Oh yeah! Will it be worth it? You betcha! Will it hurt? Probably! Will you miss the chains and the lifestyle you are leaving behind? Highly unlikely! Will this be the greatest adventure of your entire life? Absolutely!

## Stop And Think!

Before we move on, let's get personal and explore some of the tough questions. Please don't skip through this too quickly. Take time to write down your personal thoughts in the journaling area below. And if you're struggling with something really difficult, send us a letter so that we can pray specifically for you. You're not alone in this journey....someone else on this little blue planet is walking your journey with you. You are not alone!

To whom (or to what) have you given control of your life?

_____

_____

_____

_____

_____

Where have you placed your hopes and dreams?

_____

_____

_____

_____

_____

How have those things let you down or disappointed you?

_____

_____

_____

_____

_____

Are you ready to give God control of your life? How does that make you feel?

_____

_____

_____

_____

_____

Why are you afraid to give God control?

_____

_____

_____

_____

What things are you most afraid to surrender to God?

_____

_____

_____

_____

STOP & THINK

Why is it so difficult to let them go?

_____

_____

_____

_____

_____

This is your moment of decision. What is your choice?

1) I choose to embrace my chains and remain in Egypt.

2) I choose to remain on the fence of indecision, not going back to Egypt and not moving forward to the Promised Land.

3) I choose to trust God and set out for the Promised Land.

If you've chosen #3, then....woohoo! Get ready for the greatest ride of your life!

## Prayer Point

Heavenly Father, You see what a mess my life is. I am tired, God. I can't run my life anymore. It's just not working out like I had hoped. Lord, You said that You have plans for me; "Plans for peace and not disaster, plans for a future filled with hope." (Jeremiah 29:11) I really want to believe in those things right now, but I'm not sure what that looks like. I know that I need to let some things go, but I really don't know how. I've been doing a bad job of controlling my life. I can't do the things I need to do.

So Lord, I want you to take control. I'm going to need help and extra grace in this process. I can't walk tall because my problems are weighing me down. My many, many sins have all caught up with me. But Lord, I really do want to try. Can You help me, please?

You said that you would "give perfect peace to those who put their trust in you." (Isaiah 26:3) That kind of peace sounds pretty good to me. I am afraid of what might become of me if I don't figure this out. I'm desperate, God. I am broken, tired, and I need to do something radically different. Please help me face the unknowns with confidence. Trust isn't always easy for me, even with You, God, but I'd like to learn to trust. Thank You for walking this journey with me, Father. I know I need help and I'm asking You to be my everything. I can't be in charge any more. I surrender my life to Your care.

In Jesus' name, Amen.

RECOVERY

# Transition Time
## Coming Out Of Egypt

Hey, friend!

Things in Egypt aren't working out as planned. It's kind of crazy, and I don't even know why. But something's killing me here. The food or water; I don't know what it is. Anyway, I need to get out of here. Hopefully I'll be able to tell you more later. I'm feeling a bit scared and lonely.

Having Second Thoughts

P.S. Here are more pictures. They are untouched photos, like before.

## Snapshots of Leaving Egypt

Hi, I'm Deanna.

I already told you about smashing my glass pipe and falling to the floor of my garage. That was the moment I knew I had to leave Egypt, but I didn't actually leave until several weeks later.

Planning my escape wasn't easy. Nobody was there to show me the way out—nobody! Everybody I knew was enslaved in Egypt, so how could they encourage me? I remember crying with a family member on the phone, telling her how I felt like I was trapped between two worlds. I was killing myself with drugs, bad relationships, anger, and unforgiveness. That was the only life I knew. She was sympathetic, but she didn't know the way out of Egypt any more than I did.

I was terrified of losing my kids by going into residential treatment, because the courts would have proof that I was an incompetent mother. The truth is, I was an incompetent mother. My children wanted and needed more from me; much more. I couldn't stay on the fence in Egypt any longer. So, I researched my options.

Even though I didn't "feel" His presence, God was my best friend during this time. He gave me favor and the strength to continue. Soon, I was accepted for treatment. I stored all my stuff and made arrangements for the kids. I was homeless, broken, confused, alone, and extremely scared. But I was even more terrified of dying back in Egypt. My boyfriend (who later became my husband), Mitch, dropped me off at a detox center with one little suitcase, and that was that.

I felt so weird being in there with people who had mental issues, people who lived under bridges, people who talked to themselves, people who sat and rocked in corners. There I was, looking like I had it all together. I was a homeowner. (I still owned the condo that my ex-husband was living in.) I had children and I could hold a good job. These people would ask me, "Why are you here?" Good question, I wondered. How did I ever come to this place? I didn't set out to be a drug-addicted, dysfunctional, incompetent mother who prostituted herself in exchange for favors. Everything inside me was screaming, Run back! You don't belong here with all these losers! But I was so tired of trying to maintain the facade. Who was I trying to kid? I was a loser, just like the rest of them. Where could I run to, anyway? I had absolutely nothing to return to. So, I stayed— at least for a while. I had some crazy yo-yo experiences going in and out of recovery. But I was determined to leave Egypt.

Leaving Egypt was a lonely experience for me. Everybody I knew was back there. After the lonely and painful haze of those blurry days cleared away, I could finally see that Jesus had been walking with me every step of the way. But at the time, I just didn't see Him.

Hi, I'm Patrick.

My decision to leave Egypt was made in a split second. It happened after one of my "little incidents" of driving under the influence. Only this incident wasn't little. I killed an innocent young woman. It's hard to describe that kind of pain and brokenness. I had nobody to blame. After falling deeply into the pit of denial, I had finally crashed into the rocky bottom of my foolish choices. I desperately wanted to get out of the hellish nightmare—but who could show me the way?

A few months later, while I was in prison, a Christian evangelist came to tell the inmates about death and life, about sin and repentance. He told us that Jesus loved us and that He died to set us free. We could receive His forgiveness and eternal life by surrendering our lives to God. I didn't need any convincing, so I fell to my knees at the altar and repented of my sins. I remember crying like a baby, begging God for mercy. And He was faithful to forgive! At that moment, I could literally feel the chains of Egypt breaking off of me. I was gloriously delivered from the bondage of drugs and alcohol, anger and violence. All the demonic strongholds of my life were broken at that altar and I walked away a new creation in Christ. "If the Son sets you free, you will be free indeed!" (John 8:36)

I had no idea that somebody was praying specifically for me during those days. Somebody was also asking the judge and the district attorney to shorten my sentence. Then somebody began corresponding with me to bring me words of life and hope. And somebody eventually came to visit me in prison. Who was my awesome somebody? The parents of the young lady whose life I had taken. I still remember when this godly couple came to visit. I expressed my sincere regret and apology for the life I had taken. And I remember the beautiful, undeserved forgiveness I received in return. I was totally amazed to hear them say in tears that although they had lost a daughter, God had now given them a son. And that son was me! Me! Can you believe it? This couple was an incredible picture of Jesus and His love!

Not everybody has such a quick escape from Egypt. I'm not sure why God chose to miraculously deliver me, when so many other people have to battle their addictions in recovery programs and counseling. But I do know with certainty that complete victory is available to everyone through the power of God. I experienced a glorious victory over the bondage of Egypt and I have never looked back.[1]

---

1  Patrick Vandenburgh, author of *A Knock on the Door* (Tate Publishing, 2008), in discussion with the author, 2008.

Hi, I'm Cris.

Leaving Egypt after all those years was the best, the most difficult, the craziest, the most desperate thing I've ever done. I'm 5'4", and I was down to 89 pounds because of my eating disorders and drug addiction. I was having massive grand mall seizures where I'd stop breathing and turn blue. Many times, emergency workers had to be called out to my home. I'd been trying to hide all my addictions, but finally I told the doctors and my husband. I told them everything. After ten years of hiding my drug addiction, I finally came clean. It was like having a 500-pound weight taken off my shoulders. My greatest fear was the greatest lie I had believed. I believed that once I told the truth, I would lose everything. All I had ever wanted was to feel fully loved. I realized that night that to be fully loved, I would have to be fully known. Instead of leaving, my husband loved me through my exit from Egypt.

The secret was out, but I still had this huge problem of detox to go through. For the past decade, I had given my body and mind massive amounts of drugs, and then I just stopped. So, I went in my room—all alone—and I just cried out to God. "Please help me!" I said. "I don't want to die, but I don't know how to live." I was just lying there, crying, when all of a sudden, in my heart I heard the still, quiet voice of God say, "It is finished." It was just that simple.

"It is finished."

I didn't know it, but at the same time, my husband was on the internet looking for rehab homes, and a close friend of mine was in the living room, praying fervently for God to rescue me. They were really afraid of how I would react, because I could be so incredibly angry, and they knew they'd have to fight to get me into treatment.

So, after I heard God's still quiet voice, I walked out of the room and simply said, "Okay. What's next?"

My husband said, "We're packing your bags and you're flying out to a Christ-centered recovery home."

I just said, "Okay." I didn't fight them. I didn't have the strength to fight. Leaving was difficult for me, because I had small children. My husband had just been ordained a month before, and the thought of a pastor's wife going to rehab didn't bring thoughts of a warm welcome from the church. I had many anger issues to deal with—anger toward my husband, but mostly anger at myself for falling so deeply into this pit. Still, I had this huge sense of relief that the secret was out and that I was moving forward. I'd dreamed for years of being clean, but I didn't know it was even possible. The beautiful thing was that the person I feared rejection from so much was the one who embraced me and set up my recovery. This was an awesome show of love to me—of God's love.

So, I flew out of state and entered the residential living program. My body was so messed up, I don't even remember flying. But I do remember being picked up by a counselor from the program. I looked at this guy and said, "I don't know how God could ever love me or forgive me." Suddenly, the very first Bible verse I had ever memorized as a child jumped into my head: "For God loved the world so much that He gave His only Son, so that whoever believes in Him should not die but have everlasting life." (John 3:16)

Immediately, I thought, "Wow! I am 'whoever.' God loves me. I get it." For me, this was my most significant step out of Egypt toward the Promised Land; when I realized that God truly did love me and that He was looking out for me. I didn't have a clue about what recovery would look like for me, but I knew that there was no going back.

Hi, I'm E.J.

This is a letter that my little brother, E.J., wrote to a recovery program about "leaving Egypt." (Deanna)

Hello, my name is Frank Martinez and I am a twenty-six-year-old addict. I'm writing this letter to you because I am unhappy with the life I've been living and not only need, but want help.

At the time, I am in prison. I'll be released in four months. I've been in and out of prison due to my addiction problem since 1995 and I'm tired of it! I want help. My plan is to get into a program that will help me; I can't do it on my own.

# It's Time to Go
## Part 1.4

There's only one way to get out of Egypt–and that is simply to GO! There won't be a good time, a convenient time, a comfortable time, a time when everyone and everything will help facilitate this step. This one is totally up to you. God has prepared a way for you to go. You must be convinced that this is what you must do to survive. The reality is that you are dying where you are. If you really want to live, or if you are just tired of fighting to die, then you must get up and go–*right now!*

The Israelites were enslaved in Egypt. Pharaoh wasn't willing to let over a million Israelite slaves go without a fight. So God sent ten terrible plagues on Egypt to convince Pharaoh. The land of Egypt was devastated by disease, pestilence, and even the death of every firstborn son in the land–including Pharaoh's!

*That night, the king, his officials, and all the other Egyptians were awakened. There was loud crying throughout Egypt, because there was not one home in which there was not a dead son. That same night the king sent for Moses and Aaron and said, "Get out, you and your Israelites! Leave my country."(*Exodus 12:30-31)

Pharaoh finally got sick of fighting God and the Israelites. He said, "*Get out of my sight!*" There was just a narrow window of time for the Israelites to escape. Because after the dust had cleared, Pharaoh regained his courage.

*When the king of Egypt was told that the people had escaped, he and his officials changed their minds and said, "What have we done? We have let the Israelites escape and we have lost them as our slaves!" The king got his war chariot and his army ready....He pursued the Israelites, who were leaving triumphantly. (*Exodus 14:5-8)

The Israelites had only taken a few steps out of Egypt when they experienced their first big opposition. Pharaoh was coming to yank them back into slavery. You'll see later how Pharaoh received what he deserved in the end. But the point is that there may only be a narrow window of opportunity to flee from Egypt. And when your opportunity comes, you must TAKE IT before the door closes again.

If your best friend were walking into a deadly trap, you would warn them, right? That's why I can't be silent about the direction your choices are taking you. The warning may upset you, but it's offered out of love. Remaining in Egypt will kill you, my friend. It will kill you on this earth and it might even kill you eternally. That's what the enemy wants to do to your soul. I desperately hope that you will see the lies that are keeping you in slavery. Jesus said that you can know the truth and the truth will set you *free*. (John 8:32)

## Run for Freedom!

Here is a word of truth: If you are not utterly sick and tired of being sick and tired *yet*, then you are not ready to leave Egypt. That's a miserable, hopeless place to be. Believe me, I know. Nothing can numb the pain or get you high anymore. Nothing makes sense. You feel barely alive, in a black cloud of death. All you want is to get loaded again and hope to die. All of this happens before you become desperate enough to do whatever it takes to get out of that hellish place.

If you are in that place of indecision today, what will it take for you to be ready to leave your destructive lifestyle? How much longer will you hurt yourself? How much worse can life get for you? One thing is certain; life *will* get worse. Life in Egypt always does. We live in denial, thinking things will get better. Meanwhile, we keep running, trying to find our way out, new ways to work the system, to manipulate, to control, to numb the pain. We run down the next dead-end street, only to learn that it's worse than the one we just left. We run from relationships, losing the only people we love. Our great achievements include more broken relationships, more financial devastation and destitution, loss of self-respect and self-esteem, loss of children, loss of a desire to live, and ultimately a loss of our own life. I've seen it happen many times.

More people lose this battle than win it.

```
EGYPTEGYPTEGYPTEGYPTEGYPT     WILDERNESS
EGYPTEGYPTEGYPTEGYPTEGYPT     WILDERNESS
EGYPTEGYPTEGYPTEGYPTEGYPT     WILDERNESS
EGYPTEGYPTEGYPTEGYPTEGYPT     WILDERNESS
EGYPTEGYPTEGYPTEGYPTEGYPT     WILDERNESS
EGYPTEGYPTEGYPTEGYPTEGYPT     WILDERNESS
EGYPTEGYPTEGYPTEGYPTEGYPT     WILDERNESS
EGYPTE                 TEGYPT
EGYPTE   You are       TEGYPT    Not many
EGYPTE    here         TEGYPT    people
EGYPTE                 TEGYPT    make it        The few
EGYPTE                 TEGYPT                   & the
EGYPTEGYPTEGYPTEGYPT   WILDERNESS              faithful
EGYPTEGYPTEGYPTEGYPTEGYPT     WILDERNESS
EGYPTEGYPTEGYPTEGYPTEGYPT     WILDERNESS
EGYPTEGYPTEGYPTEGYPTEGYPT     WILDERNESS
EGYPTEGYPTEGYPTEGYPTEGYPT     WILDERNESS
EGYPTEGYPTEGYPTEGYPTEGYPT     WILDERNESS
EGYPTEGYPTEGYPTEGYPTEGYPT     WILDERNESS
EGYPTEGYPTEGYPTEGYPTEGYPT     WILDERNESS
EGYPTEGYPTEGYPTEGYPTEGYPT     WILDERNESS
EGYPTEGYPTEGYPTEGYPTEGYPT     WILDERNESS
EGYPTEGYPTEGYPTEGYPTEGYPT     WILDERNESS
```

P
R
O
M
I
S
E
D

L
A
N
D

*Jesus said, "Enter through the narrow gate because the gate and road that lead to destruction are wide. Many enter through the wide gate. But the narrow gate and the road that lead to life are full of trouble. Only a few people find the narrow gate."* (Matthew 7:13-14)

The few and the faithful find their way to the Promised Land. Tragically, many people die in Egypt. They entertain the idea of escape, but never actually take the plunge. Others make it out of denial and admit they are dying in Egypt. They see through the lies of the lifestyle and the mindset that keeps them in bondage. They make a commitment to get out. They run like hell, fast and furious, understanding that this door of opportunity will not remain open forever. They understand that they are in the middle of a battle–a spiritual battle that requires them to run for their lives. They learn to quit fighting against people and things. They realize that the weapons of this war are spiritual. They believe that God can take the pieces of their broken lives and salvage them. They trust that He will make it right again somehow.

## It's Not That Complicated

We tend to complicate our decision to leave a destructive lifestyle. We play scenes of the past in our heads over and over again, naively believing that the future will somehow be better. We foolishly talk about the "good old days," forgetting how bad they really were. We look at ourselves in the mirror and we can't stand what we see. We can't even look ourselves in the eyes anymore. We want to run, hide, and die in a cave somewhere because of what our life has become. And we're not even sure how it got to this point. But the reality is, it did. We try to justify ourselves by blaming others. But it doesn't matter who is to blame. Look ahead, not behind. The decision to leave Egypt is one that only *you* can make. Nobody else can make it for you.

The fact is that you are in this hellish hole. Your parents can't get you out. Your friends can't get you out. The government can't get you out. Winning the lottery won't get you out. There is only one way out!

The truth is that Jesus has made a way for you to get out. The keys to unlock your prison cell are right in front of you. Freedom is just ahead. Will you take the keys and walk out of your prison? No one can make you do this. It doesn't matter where you are in life. It doesn't matter who is doing what to you, or what you are doing to yourself. This freedom begins in the secret place of your heart, and nobody on earth can keep you imprisoned. Only you can keep yourself there. This is your choice. This is your Day of Salvation, right here, right now.

*But what does it say? "The word is near you; it is in your mouth and in your heart,"* *that is, the word of faith we are proclaiming: That if you confess with your mouth,* *"Jesus is Lord," and believe in your heart that God raised him from the dead, you* *will be saved. For it is with your heart that you believe and are justified, and it is* *with your mouth that you confess and are saved. As the Scripture says, "Anyone* *who trusts in him will never be put to shame."*(Romans 10:8-11, NIV)

No matter where you are or where you've been, God wants you to live a life that is beautiful, effective, abundant, and free. Will you immediately be free from pain and trouble if you decide to run from Egypt? No, that's not how it goes. God is much more concerned with our character than He is our comfort. It takes time and energy to get out of bondage, but it is totally worth it. The more you trust Him, the more supernatural help He'll give you. Before you know it, what used to be hard for you will come easily.

The decision to leave Egypt does not mean that you have to be perfect. If you had to be good and worthy before you left, nobody would ever leave. It's not possible. Holy living comes as we walk with God and follow His teachings.  But that lifestyle comes *after* the decision to leave Egypt, not before. Today is the day for making a decision to leave. It's that simple. Once you have made the decision and set your heart on the pilgrimage to a different course in life, God will give you strength day by day to live out the decision. You have to catch a fish before you can clean it— right? God starts cleaning our hearts, as soon as we confess that we need His help. As long as we are willing, He is able.

*The steadfast love of the Lord never ceases. His mercies never come to an end; they are new every morning; great is thy faithfulness. (*Lamentations 3:22-23, RSV*)*

*Forgetting the past and looking forward to what lies ahead, I strain to reach the end of the race and receive the prize.(*Philippians 3:13-14*)*

*Blessed are those whose strength is in you, who have the set their hearts on pilgrimage. (Psalms 84:5, NIV)*

*I know that through your prayers and the help given by the Spirit of Jesus Christ, what has happened to me will turn out for my deliverance. I eagerly expect and hope that I will in no way be ashamed, but will have sufficient courage so that now as always Christ will be exalted in my body, whether by life or by death. (*Philippians 1:19-20*)*

*Come to me all who are weary and heavy laden, and I will give you rest. (*Matthew 11:28*)*

*You give glory to my Father when you produce a lot of fruit and therefore show that you are my disciples. (John 15:8)*

*A thief comes to steal, kill, and destroy. But I came so that my sheep will have life and so that they will have everything they need. (John 10:10)*

These Bible verses are about the journey. God wants you to know that you are not alone. Maybe you believe that nobody cares what happens to you, but that is just not true. God cares for you and so do believers, just like me, all over the world. *We are the Body!* We are the Body of Christ, and He has His people strategically placed everywhere. If you have asked Him to save you, then you have supernatural help at your disposal already. God will send out His laborers to help you.

I already mentioned that leaving Egypt was one of the loneliest times of my life. I had nobody to encourage me, to cheer me on, to tell me that I could rise above the things that were killing me. But God loved me and He was walking with me, even if I didn't know it at the time. He will walk with you, too. When we can't feel God's presence, we cannot be ruled by our emotions and think that He is not there. He is. He is continually working on our behalf with a forward-moving mind toward us. He continually looks ahead and provides ways for us to arrive where He already sees us. He sends new people into our lives and opens new doors for us to walk through. If you are lacking an earthly cheering section, *don't get discouraged!* You have angels all around you that are cheering you on. *Praise Jesus!*

*Are not all angels ministering spirits sent to serve those who will inherit salvation?* (Hebrews 1:14, NIV)

There are so many excuses for deciding to stay in Egypt, but I pray that you will squash each one. Maybe you've tried and failed before. That's no excuse! Today is a new day. Hope is ahead, not behind. You might be thinking that it's impossible to let go of everything from the past at one time. It's not a problem. Let go of whatever you can, and start walking. You should know, however, that the more junk you leave behind today, the lighter your load will be, and the easier your journey will become. It's hard to let go of our past pains, disappointments, frustrations, and resentments. It's difficult to shed our addictions, bad habits, and bad relationships overnight. It's easier to take you out of Egypt than it is to take Egypt out of you. That takes more time. But God is not asking you to get everything accomplished in a day. He only wants you to take a few simple steps in the right direction.

You are standing at the crossroads. The road before you leads to life; the one behind you leads to death. You determine what baggage you will take with you. Maybe you're not ready to let go of all the abuse you've suffered, to grieve the life you didn't have, to understand your abandonment, to deal with a lifetime of regrets. If you can't let go of those things right now, that's okay. Simply take that first step out of bondage and trust that God will make a way for the rest. The power of heaven is at your disposal!

Are you prepared to go now? Please remember that you are not alone. So many precious travelers like you have made this journey. They are standing with you, and cheering you on. We have traveled the road before you and with God's help we can guide you through. Will you trust Him in the days ahead? Will you trust that He has a plan for you? Will you trust Him to make your steps safe and good? Will you watch Him light the way for you in the darkness?

*Planning Your Escape*

Here's a simple plan for your escape:

Trust

Surrender

Choose

Let Go!

**Trust** is something that you can do! You already have trusted others and you have trusted yourself. You've trusted in your ability to get yourself out of trouble and it hasn't worked. So why not put that trust in God, instead? How? Just get down on your knees and say, "God, I have made a decision today. I am putting my trust in you!" When you release faith-filled words to God, it puts heaven into motion. He will never fail you.

**Surrender** is nothing new to you. You have already surrendered yourself to your addictions, your habits, the expectations of others, and to toxic relationships. Why not surrender your life to the One who loves you and who can free you from bondage? Say, "I surrender myself to You, God!"

**Choose** life or choose death. You have chosen a lifestyle that is killing you. Maybe you've even chosen to give up fighting and die. That's where I was when I finally decided to leave Egypt. Now, choose to trust God. Choose to surrender to His wonderful plan for your life. Choose to allow God to show you the way. Choose to take His advice in the journey ahead. Choose to seek His direction and follow. Say, "Show me the way, God." When you agree with God about your sin, when you trust, surrender, and make a choice to include God in your life, that's called repentance. Look what happens up in heaven when you send God some knee-mail:

*I tell you that in the same way there will be more rejoicing in heaven over one sinner who repents than over ninety-nine righteous persons who do not need to repent. (Luke 15:7, NIV)*

When we trust, surrender, and choose God, it stirs things up in heaven. If you look up the word "rejoice" in the dictionary it says, "to welcome, to enjoy, and to be glad." You should never feel alone after reading that Scripture–you are now plugged into the Kingdom of Heaven! Nothing we can do will get past God, Jesus, the saints who have died before us, and the angels in heaven—*Wow!*

**Let go** of everything that is keeping you from accomplishing and experiencing the abundant life God has for you. Can you do that? I believe you can. If God can help someone like me, I believe with all my heart He can and will do the same for you. I believe in you. Acts 10:34 says that God is no respecter of persons. In other words, His gift of salvation is free to anyone who asks.

*Dear Jesus, I know I am a sinner. I am trying hard to believe that God loves me. Because of Your unbelievable and unconditional love for me, You were born, crucified, and rose again for the forgiveness of my sins. Not just so that I can have the assurance of going to heaven one day, but also so that I may be free here and now. I accept that you are the Son of God and my one and only hope of salvation. I ask You, Jesus, to come into my heart and to be my Lord and Savior. I ask that You might help me to walk in relationship with You as my life is transformed and I become the new creation that You say I can be. I thank You that my sins are forgiven and that I am offered a new life through You from this day forward. I give You my heart and my life, and I ask that You take the throne and show me how to live a better life, day by day. In Your name I pray, Amen.*

## Stop And Think!

Are you really ready to leave Egypt? If so, how do you know?

_____

_____

_____

_____

_____

If you are not ready to go; what is stopping you? What else has to happen for you to be ready?

_____

_____

_____

_____

What will be the hardest thing to leave behind?

_____

_____

_____

_____

Where have you placed your trust in the past?

_____

_____

_____

_____

_____

How have these things failed you?

_____

_____

_____

_____

What must you surrender in order to move forward out of Egypt?

_____

_____

_____

_____

_____

What does letting go look like for you? Specifically, what can you do right now?

_____

_____

_____

_____

_____

## Prayer Point

Heavenly Father, I am tired. I can't stay here any longer. I really want to get out of Egypt. I need Your help, Lord. I can't make it alone. I know that many have traveled this road before me. Yet, I am still having a hard time believing that You will help me out of here. I really don't have anywhere else to turn. Please help me, Father. There are so many things from my past that are a heavy burden for me. I can't carry them, and yet I can't seem to let go of them, either. Please help me, Lord, to live a lighter life, free from these burdens and pains.

Help me know how to walk this journey of my life one day at a time. I am starting to believe that Your grace is sufficient. Thank You for showing me Your love and grace even when I doubt You. Please continue to be with me, Lord, as I make the next tough steps out of Egypt. Help me to grow as You give me the strength to get Egypt out of my system. Help me, Father, to run and not look back. Thank You for saving me and not letting me die. Help me to live the best I can with this second, third, fourth, hundredth chance You've given me. Thanks for sending friends to walk with me, even if I haven't met those friends yet. Thanks for never giving up on me.

In Jesus' Name, Amen.

# Deliverance: God's Invitation Out
## Part 1.5

In the book of Exodus, God not only wanted to deliver Moses from slavery, He also wanted Moses to lead many other Israelites out of slavery. That was Moses' divine purpose. Unfortunately, his purpose was derailed by his own naivety.

Moses went to see his own people and watched them suffering under forced labor. He saw a Hebrew, one of his own people, being beaten by an Egyptian. He looked all around, and when he didn't see anyone, he beat the Egyptian to death and hid the body in the sand. When Pharaoh heard what Moses had done, he tried to have him killed. But Moses fled from Pharaoh and settled in the land of Midian. After a long time passed, the king of Egypt died. The Israelites still groaned because they were slaves. So they cried out, and their cries for help went up to God. God heard their groaning, and he remembered his promise to Abraham, Isaac, and Jacob. (Exodus 2:11-24)

Moses spent forty years in Midian before God brought him back to rescue the Israelites from slavery. Forty wasted years! How many years have you wasted? Some of us make bad decisions and end up in the wilderness of recovery, prison or treatment. Like Moses, God hasn't forgotten us. He still loves us and He still wants to lead us back into His will, back toward deliverance. He is calling you, just like he called Moses in the Midian desert.

*The Messenger of the Lord appeared to Moses there [in Midian] as flames of fire coming out of a bush. Moses looked, and although the bush was on fire, it was not burning up.  Then God called to him from the bush, "Moses, Moses!" Moses answered, "Here I am!"  The Lord said, "I have seen the misery of my people in Egypt, and I have heard them crying out because of the slave drivers. I know how much they're suffering ... Now, go! I am sending you to Pharaoh so that you can bring my people Israel out of Egypt."(Exodus 3:1-10)*

Like Moses, we must trust God's plan for our lives. We must be obedient and diligent to follow it, even if we do not understand it. We also must be prepared for opposition from the king we have been serving. Satan will not let us go without a fight.

*Later Moses and Aaron went to Pharaoh and said, "This is what the Lord God of Israel says: 'Let my people go.'" Pharaoh asked, "Who is the Lord? Why should I obey Him and let Israel go? I don't know the Lord, and I won't let Israel go." That same day Pharaoh gave these orders to the slave drivers and foremen, "Make the work harder for these people."* (Exodus 5:1-9)

God had made it clear that it was time for His people to go. God gave Moses boldness to speak to Pharaoh. Today, He gives *you* the same boldness to speak out against the things that enslave you. By *the authority of God* we are to command the devil, "Let me go!" But we can also expect his opposition, because he's had us under his thumb for so long. He will say, "Why should I let you go? I *won't* let you go. Now work harder for me!"

The devil knows that he doesn't stand a chance against God. He also knows we have the authority to cast him out in Jesus' name. That's why it is so important not to give up when the intensity of the battle increases. Trust me – the more you put God's Word into practice, the stronger your faith gets. The devil is forced to submit to God's power in your life.

What would have happened if Moses and Aaron had just said, "Okay, You're right. We'll all go back to work. Sorry to bother you, Pharaoh. We'll even work a little extra overtime to make up for the interruption." Oh no! Moses and Aaron expected opposition and it came, all right. Expect a battle when you decide to get out of slavery.

## A Future Filled With Hope

Sometimes the devil tries to convince us that God has planned our destruction; that it's God's will for us to be in ruin. The truth is that God is heartbroken about your suffering. He is waiting for you to step into the Wilderness. He is yearning for you to take the wonderful promises He has offered you.

*I know the plans that I have for you, declares the Lord. They are plans for peace and not disaster, plans to give you a future filled with hope.* (Jeremiah 29:11)

God's incredible plans for us can even survive our bad choices. Jesus has been with us from start to finish. He watched us make those bad decisions, and He has wept over us. He wept over all the painful things others have done to us and that we have done to others. He did not plan for us to be abused, rejected, abandoned, and betrayed. But He allows each one of us to make our own choices. He allows us to run *to* Him or *from* Him. He is waiting patiently to share His merciful healing plans with you.

Now, let's look at how Moses got angry at God for Pharaoh's response:

*Moses went back to the Lord and asked, "Why have you brought this trouble on your people? Why did you send me? Ever since I went to Pharaoh to speak for you, he has treated your people cruelly, and you have done nothing at all to rescue your people." (Exodus 5:22-23)*

Wow! He was really mad! Moses poured his heart out to God–just as we should do *all* the time. Notice how Moses expresses his questions and frustrations to God. I'm surprised he's talking to God like that. Well, not really, since I have talked to God like that myself. Maybe you have, too. But here's a truth I've learned through my many times of questioning: God isn't intimated by our honesty, our tantrums, or our unbelief. God prefers our candid confessions of how we feel. He's a loving Father who wants us to bring these matters to Him. He's not shocked, because He already knows how we feel. In fact, it brings Him joy when we cry out to Him, because He's the only One who can truly help us. It's better than punching walls or kicking dogs, don't you think?

Listen to how God responded to Moses' prayer:

*Then the Lord said to Moses, "Now you will see what I will do to Pharaoh. I will show him my power, and he will let my people go. I will show him my power, and he will throw them out of his country." God spoke to Moses, "I am the Lord. I appeared to Abraham, Isaac, and Jacob as God Almighty, but I didn't make myself known to them by my name, the Lord. I even made a promise to give them Canaan, the land where they lived as foreigners. Now I have heard the groaning of the Israelites, whom the Egyptians hold in slavery, and I have remembered my promise.*

*"Tell the Israelites, 'I am the Lord. I will bring you out from under the oppression of the Egyptians, and I will free you from slavery. I will rescue you with my powerful arm and with mighty acts of judgment. Then I will make you my people, and I will be your God. You will know that I am the Lord your God, who brought you out from under the forced labor of the Egyptians. I will bring you to the land I solemnly swore to give to Abraham, Isaac, and Jacob. I will give it to you as your own pos-*

*session. I am the Lord.'"*

*Moses reported this to the Israelites. But they would not listen to him because they were so discouraged by their back-breaking work. Then the Lord spoke to Moses, "Go tell Pharaoh (the king of Egypt) to let the Israelites leave his country." But Moses protested to the Lord, "The Israelites wouldn't listen to me. Why would Pharaoh listen to me? I'm such a poor speaker." The Lord spoke to Moses and Aaron about the Israelites and Pharaoh (the king of Egypt). He commanded them to bring the Israelites out of Egypt. (Exodus 6:1-13)*

Is it God's plan for you to remain in Egypt, or to take the difficult journey to the Promised Land? Based on what we learn from these verses in Exodus, God says to you:

1) I will free you from bondage.

2) Believe that what I say is true. I am not like a man who lies.

3) Wait, watch, and see what I will do to the one who has kept you bound. The devil will pay for what he has done to My precious children.

4) I promised Abraham, Isaac, and Jacob a long time ago that their descendants would be free. I have been planning good things for you for a long time.

5) I love and accept you because you are My child.

6) Do not allow your discouragement to be so strong that you stop believing in My promises for your life.

7) You may feel weak, but you are not helpless. My strength is more than enough to release you from bondage.

What happened next in the story of Exodus? All hell broke loose. The king of Egypt made life difficult for the Israelites, and God made life difficult for the Egyptians by sending plagues. Does that craziness sound familiar? Oh yeah, you bet! When we finally make the decision to leave, it seems like everything blows to pieces. Just when we think life couldn't get any worse….suddenly it does.

I don't know what devastation has fallen on your life. For the people in Egypt, it was water turning to blood, frogs, gnats, flies, dead animals, sores, hailstones, grasshoppers, and darkness. You might be feeling more hopeless than ever, but don't be discouraged. God is at work. When a war is waging for your soul, things are going to get a little crazy for a while. God's good plan is for you to find freedom, not to die in Egypt. But the devil isn't going to give you up without a fight. Just keep your eyes focused on Jesus. He will instruct you in how to survive. Listen to Him!

God wants us to be free–radically transformed; absolutely free; even unrecognizable to those who once knew us as slaves in Egypt. We have God's promises and a covenant written in His Son's own blood! These promises are like legal contracts that He will not break. He's not "wishy washy" like man; God is steadfast and sure! He plans to lead us right out of slavery and into a glorious life of freedom.

So what do you think, my friend? Can you trust His plan and follow His road map, even when all hell breaks loose?

## Stop And Think!

Are you convinced yet that it is time to get out of Egypt and get the Egypt out of you? If not, then what do you believe is better than God's promise of life and freedom?

_____

_____

_____

_____

_____

What are God's plans for you? Do you believe His plans?

_____

_____

_____

_____

_____

What specifically are you afraid of? Is God big enough to conquer those fears?

_____

_____

_____

_____

_____

What lies are preventing you from believing God's plans for you? What does the Word of God say about each one of those lies?

_____

_____

_____

_____

_____

What have you blamed God for in the past? What anger have you had toward Him? Can you speak your complaints honestly to God today and if possible, confess that His plans for you are good?

_____

_____

_____

_____

_____

Have you seen God working difficult circumstances out in your life? How?

_____

_____

_____

_____

_____

STOP & THINK

Do you believe that you are too weak to leave Egypt? Can you confess this weakness to God today, and commit to lean on His strength?

_____

_____

_____

_____

_____

Describe your feelings about God's invitation into the wilderness:

_____

_____

_____

_____

_____

_____

_____

_____

_____

_____

STOP & THINK

## Prayer Point

God, I often wonder why I go around the same mountain so many times. Have I not learned that You will never leave me nor forsake me? Do I not yet understand that Your love is the true love my heart longs for? Lord, I need you. Not like I need friends or money. I really need You. Without You, I am lost and I am nothing. Through my desperation, I know that You are all I need. Once again, I find myself broken at Your feet, asking for Your love to make me complete. All I need is You. Help is on the way, because You're coming to me. All I know is that I need You, Jesus.

Almighty God, I withdraw from the things of this world, from the things around me; into a place of solitude. Jesus, even as You went to a quiet place to escape from the noisy crowds and into the wilderness to be alone with God, so I withdraw into the Wilderness, and there I seek Your face and Your voice. What I pray for in secret You will reward openly. Father, I lay aside the things of this earth so that I can just be with You. Like You, Jesus, I want nothing except the Father's will for me. Just You and me, Father. I look to your face. Deliver me, Daddy. Get me out of here. I'm done living in Egypt.

In Jesus' Name, Amen.

# Leaving Isn't Easy
## Part 1.6

*Go in through the narrow gate. The gate to destruction is wide, and the road that leads there is easy to follow. A lot of people go through that gate. (*Matthew 7:13, CEV*)*

Here you are. You've taken your first steps out of Egypt. But you're running, because the enemy is hot on your trail. Like the Israelites, it feels like your former master might chase you all the way to the Red Sea. You might think you are running into a trap and there's nowhere else to go. But there is. Keep running straight ahead and you'll find yourself in the arms of your Heavenly Father. Do you hear Him calling you? Trust His voice. He will make a way when things look hopeless. Trust Him. Every one of us who has fled from Egypt has walked that same road. We're cheering you on, and so is heaven!

Again, you have three choices:

1) Go back to where you were dying to leave;
2) Stay right where you are and die in your indecision; or
3) keep moving forward.

Go for it! What do you have to lose? You know that all the junk of Egypt is worth nothing. What do you have to gain? You have *everything* to gain! And you can do it. You can do all things through Christ who strengthens you. (Philippians 4:13) You have come too far to go back now. Besides, your enemy is right at your heels. Don't go back, or he will grind you to pieces. Get out of here before it's too late. Jesus has cleared the way before you. He is calling you. Take the narrow road, where abundant life is waiting for you. You will never regret it.

The journey can seem difficult if you dwell on the things that you are leaving behind: an abusive relationship or years of addiction. You may have to confront the anger and unforgiveness in your heart so that you can walk free. You might have to let go of your right to play victim or martyr. You may have to leave behind toxic relationships, or ungodly beliefs and lies that the enemy has told you. You might have to walk away from your self-sufficiency to learn to depend on God. Like me, you may have to walk away from everyone and everything for a season. That's okay. God will help you sort through your thoughts and desires. He'll show you what is good and what is bad. He'll help you bring the good back into your life. It will be much better than you ever imagined; but only after you surrender your life into His hands.

## Hope Lies Ahead

First, you have to lay some things down. You might have to lay down guilt and shame for the sins of your past, or for the sins of others who have wronged you. Can you hear the sound of water parting? It's the sound of God making a way for you to run for your life. The waves are crashing all around you, and yet God has promised that you will not drown if you stand in His perfect peace. "In all your ways acknowledge Him and He will make your path straight." (Proverbs 3:6) You can't see down the road far enough to know exactly what you are running into, but hopefully, you have determined that running is better than dying in Egypt. That's all you really need to know at this point.

Leaving is never easy. It's even hard to walk away from a life of total insanity. I remember all the crazy feelings; knowing I couldn't keep my life the way it was, and yet I didn't have the nerve to leave the only world I had ever known. How could I survive if my world was turned upside down and inside out? I was so afraid of the unknown. One of the hardest things was letting go of my control. In reality, my life was totally *out of control*–thanks to nobody but me. But at least I knew what to expect. At that point, I was faithless. I wasn't plugged into heaven's power. When I cried out to God in my garage that day, He released His power into my life.

Maybe you, too, are thinking: *Step out into the unknown? What the….are you serious? I don't have a clue what that will look like. I can't just take a leap of faith and freefall out into the great abyss of who-knows-what? That's absurd!*

I'm sure that's what the Israelites were thinking when they were trapped between Pharaoh's army and the edge of the Red Sea.

Here's what happened just as they were leaving Egypt:

*After the king had finally let the people go, the Lord did not lead them through Philistine territory, though that was the shortest way. God had said, "If they are attacked, they may decide to return to Egypt." So he led them around through the desert and toward the Red Sea. The Israelites left Egypt prepared for battle.* (Exodus 13:17-18, CEV)

The Lord led the Israelites in the way that was best for them. Did you know that God also has been trying to lead you to life and freedom? Maybe that's why you are reading this book....

God will not necessarily take you the easy or short way. He will take you the way that He knows will lead to your lasting victory. It is for this reason that I often find it difficult to pray with someone whose request is to get out of prison early. Not that I don't believe God reduces sentences, because I do. And not that I haven't hoped and prayed that people I know and love would be pardoned or released early. But let's be honest–we're not nearly as smart as God. We may think we know what is best for us. But what is most convenient, comfortable, quickest or most efficient is not always God's best for us. We're like a butterfly fighting its way out of the cocoon. If a compassionate person came along, saw the struggle, and helped the butterfly out, it would die. That struggle is what gives the butterfly its strength to live.

God knows that if we go the easy way, we will be attacked and we might return to Egypt. Why would God allow us to get out of Egypt quickly if He knows we will just fall right back into deeper trouble? Don't get mad at Him for causing you to take a slower path, such as staying in prison longer. God leads us in the direction we are to go and He works things out in His perfect timing.

The Bible says that "the Israelites left Egypt prepared for battle," although they never had to fight. Isn't that like us? We worry and fret over all the worst-case scenarios. We rehearse in our minds the millions of things that can go wrong, but how many of them actually happen? The majority of things I stressed over never happened. The other problems that God allowed, I didn't have to worry about. Why not? Just like the Israelites, your battle belongs to the Lord. Once you accept Jesus as your personal Lord and Savior, you become God's responsibility. He fights for you, so no worries!

## Between the Devil and the Deep Blue Sea

So there the Israelites stood, trapped between the devil and the deep blue sea. With thousands of soldiers closing in on them, God already had planned their escape. The Israelites were so busy complaining, they didn't even notice. It's amazing that even though God had performed miracle after miracle to get them to this place, they doubted Him.

*They also complained to Moses, "Wasn't there enough room in Egypt to bury us? Is that why you brought us out here to die in the desert? Why did you bring us out of Egypt anyway? While we were there, didn't we tell you to leave us alone? We would rather be slaves in Egypt than die in this desert!" But Moses answered, "Don't be afraid! Be brave, and you will see the Lord save you today. These Egyptians will never bother you again. The Lord will fight for you, and you won't have to do a thing." The Lord said to Moses, "Why do you keep calling out to me for help? Tell the Israelites to move forward."* (Exodus 14:11-16)

Isn't that like you and me? We get so far. We are so close to our breakthrough. We're standing at the brink of our miracle. Then, when the going gets tough, we shake our fist at God and say, *"What's the matter with You? Why did You bring me here to die?"* We begin to think that life back in Egypt was better than where we imagine God is taking us.

I love what God said to the Israelites at that point. It's the same thing He says to you today:

*Move forward.*

It's just that simple. Don't grumble and worry when God has everything figured out. He is saying, "I have already made the way, My child. Now step into it. Move forward. You must take the step and allow Me to destroy the evil powers that have been tormenting you. Don't be afraid! Be brave and watch Me save you. Your chains will fall from you and turn to dust under your feet. I am the Lord who will fight for you. Yes, you are weak, but I am strong and mighty. Don't keep standing there with that worried look on your face. Trust me! You said that you would."

**Move forward!**

**Believe to Receive by Deanna Allen**

The Bible is packed with God's promises.
These promises are for you and for me.
But not all of the promises of God,
Will we immediately get to feel or see.

Many of the promises of God,
Are worked in us over time.
Sometimes God has to remove things,
Things that can block our heart or mind.

We have to trust God's Word,
Believe, believe, and believe.
The measure of our faith,
Can determine how much we receive.

When we're standing on a promise,
And we're watching and waiting and praying;
Are we standing firm on our word from God?
Or are we shaken by what our circumstances are saying?

Without faith it's impossible to please God,
And faith without works is dead.
Stand on your promise with faith and assurance.
Don't doubt what our awesome God said.

Let's look at how that part of the story ends:

*Moses held out his hand over the sea, and the Lord drove the sea back with a strong east wind. It blew all night and turned the sea into dry land. The water was divided, and the Israelites went through the sea on dry ground, with walls of water on both sides. The Egyptians pursued them and went after them into the sea with all their horses, chariots, and drivers. Just before dawn the Lord looked down....at the Egyptian army and threw them into a panic. He made the wheels of their chariots get stuck, so that they moved with great difficulty. The Egyptians said, "The Lord is fighting for the Israelites against us. Let's get out of here!"*

*The Lord said to Moses, "Hold out your hand over the sea, and the water will come back over the Egyptians and their chariots and drivers." So Moses held out his hand over the sea, and at daybreak the water returned to its normal level. The Egyptians tried to escape from the water, but the Lord threw them into the sea. The water returned and covered the chariots, the drivers, and all the Egyptian army that had followed the Israelites into the sea; not one of them was left. But the Israelites walked through the sea on dry ground, with walls of water on both sides ... When the Israelites saw the great power with which the Lord had defeated the Egyptians, they stood in awe of the Lord; and they had faith in the Lord and in his servant Moses.(Exodus 14:21-31)*

# The Wilderness
## Part 2

Hey, there, friend.

What a crazy journey this has become.
Indescribable! Man, it's lonely here
in the desert. Sometimes I feel like
I'm the only one on this God-forsaken
planet. Remember the "good old" days?
They had to be better than this.

Feeling Lost and Forgotten

P.S. I have a few photos
to send you of the
Wilderness, but I don't
have the software to
"touch up" these pictures.
So, unfortunately, you're
seeing the real deal.

## Snapshots of the Wilderness

Hi, I'm Deanna.

Walking out of Egypt was one of the most difficult times of my life. Loneliness and discouragement were my closest companions. Satan kept telling me, "You're not good enough. You're going to fail. You're doing this for nothing. Even if you get through this recovery program, you're still worthless. They'll take your kids away and you'll go home to nothing. The only good thing is that your kids will be better off without you. You're nothing but a lonely loser out in this wilderness."

It's true that I was lonely, and I was certainly a loser. I failed at my first few residential rehab attempts. I actually went through four different centers before I finally got sober! My transition out of Egypt took many months because of my pride, insecurity, anger, and relationship addictions. So if you have a hard time getting out of Egypt, don't give up. It's not the end of the road, just because you stumble and fall once or twice. "A righteous person may fall seven times, but he gets up again." (Proverbs 24:16) My failures and frustrations were showing me how utterly helpless I was. They showed me that I couldn't even trust people for my recovery. These obstacles caused me to fall totally into the arms of Jesus.

I fully and completely dedicated my life to Jesus Christ. I said, "You are God. I've been making up my own gods all along, and it has been a dismal failure. Forgive me, Jesus. I'm laying my life completely in Your hands. I can't do this anymore. I surrender. There's not much left of my broken life, but You can have it all."

Jesus took my broken life, and bit by bit, He began to reassemble it and make something beautiful out of it. That took time, of course. But the important thing was that I finally let go of all the things I'd been clinging to so tightly. Jesus is a gentleman. He waited for me to willingly surrender my life to Him.

*Hi, I'm Michelle.*

*I never thought I would do it, but I actually left Egypt! I was raised by an abusive alcoholic. I had been stuck in a life of drugs, alcohol, abuse, sexual addictions, and self-injury. I anticipated living in my pit until I died, just like everyone else in my family. I accepted the fact that my life was meant to be that way, and I just needed to be a big girl and cope with it. Then God got ahold of me, and I'm sure glad He did.*

*At first, I rejected the idea of going to a residential treatment center that was miles away from home. God finally convinced me that this was what He wanted, so I gave up my job, my apartment, my car, and my furniture. I put what was left into storage, and I even gave away my cat. I left my family and friends behind. God stripped me of literally everything. I felt like I was placing the only thing left into His hands—my life!*

*In the Wilderness, I clung to the hope that leaving everything behind was the right choice and that life would get better. I didn't understand how that could happen, but I believed that God did. He called me to a Wilderness where I was a perfect stranger. I didn't even know how long I would be there. I had so many questions: What will happen, Lord? What will I do without an income and without my stuff? What will I do without a job? How will I survive? God's answer was always the same: "Just trust me."*

*During that time, God gave me a promise from Scripture to stand on. He called Abram to leave everything, with the promise that he would receive incredible blessings one day. God said, "Leave your land, your relatives, and your father's home. Go to the land that I will show you. I will make you a great nation. I will bless you. I will make your name great, and you will be a blessing." (Genesis 12:1-2) I held onto that Scripture from the moment I applied for the rehab program. It carried me through the Wilderness, and I have not let go of it since. I can still hear God's voice encouraging me. "Just trust me."*

Hi, I'm E.J.

Life here in San Quentin is … well, same ol', same ol'. When I think back on the times when I was improving, I wonder what happened to the person I was then. For a short time, I actually felt like it was okay to feel like everything mattered. I found that I actually wanted my loved ones to have expectations of me; to want the best from me. Before, I had always run from that. I told myself that I was just a clown as deep as a dinner plate. Maybe I was afraid that if I tried to be more; I'd fail. It's a fact that if you don't try, you can't fail—foolproof! I didn't promise anyone anything, other than perhaps a good time. When I was drunk or loaded and did any of the stupid and embarrassing things that have cost me my friends and my self-esteem, no one could be disappointed.

But then, a funny thing happened. I found out that the more I acknowledged how much I cared, the better my life became. I started actually trying all of the time, in a hundred different ways, and I stunned myself by succeeding! Some of my core bedrock had shifted and settled. I could take down my guard, breathe, and enjoy. I don't know what it was about my hardwiring that had made me fear commitment so much, but gradually, the life I was living at home with my family became the only thing I really wanted in the whole world.[1]

 1 John Lescroart, *The First Law* (New York: Penguin Books, 2003), 409-410.

Hi, I'm Cris.

My twenty-eight days in residential treatment were like boot camp for my body, soul, and mind. It was there that I met my God and Savior on a personal level. In my brokenness, I learned how to love myself. But I still had all other kinds of baggage and confusion. I was kind of like one of the slaves emancipated after the American Civil War. The slaves were told they were free, but many didn't have a clue what that meant. Where were they supposed to go? What were they supposed to do? Slavery was all they knew. That was me. I was delivered after ten years of addiction, but I didn't know what freedom was. I had a lifetime of habits, hurts, and hang-ups that I still needed to work through. I didn't have a clue how to be a wife and mother or a friend. I spent the first few months home by hanging out at a friend's house, talking, talking, and talking. I went to recovery meetings daily and stayed away from my husband and small children.

Egypt was chaos for me, but the Wilderness brought order to my life. I spent a lot of time at home when my husband was at work and kids were at school. I had to learn basic life skills. I remember looking at my family for the first time after I had arrived home. I wondered "Who are these people?" I had to learn to live all over again. I wrote to-do lists to take out the trash; check the mailbox, make lunches for my kids; all kinds of simple tasks. Those were things I had lost in my abuse and addiction. I did them mechanically, with a sense of duty, but in time, that duty was replaced by true love for and devotion to my family. It was a beautiful thing.

I still had huge self-esteem issues and despised who I was. Through counseling, I dissected every part of my past. This was serious stuff, when you add up all the years of rape, molestation, cutting, drugs, bulimia, and hypocrisy. Every time I went *into counseling, it felt like I was getting beaten. It was like stepping into a boxing ring with Satan. I knew I was going to win because of God's authority, but it hurt so much. I'd walk away victorious, but totally exhausted. I found miraculous healing—not just by revisiting my past, but by lifting my past up to Jesus and asking Him to set me free from all that pain and bondage.*

*I also found tremendous freedom by getting rid of my religious performance in front of my church friends. I learned to stop hiding my problems. Instead, I'd boast about my weaknesses (like the Apostle Paul did). I cried with the pastor's wife. I told her how I sucked at being a wife and mother, how I sucked at being a good Christian. It was extremely liberating, and it helped me to rely so much more on God's strength—the truth will set you free!*

*My whole perspective on life was changing. I previously had such a distorted view of life; I was like a little girl seeing the world through a window that had been shattered into a million pieces. All of God's beautiful creations looked like monsters through that window. Suddenly, God replaced that window with crystal-clear glass, and it was remarkable. That change in perspective didn't happen overnight, but it happened. That's the miracle of my recovery.*

# Wandering in the Wilderness
## Part 2.1

## Grumble, Grumble

Let's look at the continuing saga of the Israelites on their journey to the Promised Land. Here's what happened immediately after God's glorious victory over Pharaoh and his army at the Red Sea:

*Miriam the prophetess, Aaron's sister, took a tambourine, and all the women followed her with tambourines, dancing. Miriam led them in singing, "Sing to God– what a victory! He pitched horse and rider into the sea!"*

*Moses led Israel from the Red Sea on to the Wilderness of Shur. They traveled for three days through the wilderness without finding any water. They got to Marah, but they couldn't drink the water at Marah; it was bitter. That's why they called the place Marah (Bitter). And the people complained to Moses, "So what are we supposed to drink?"*

*So Moses cried out in prayer to God. God pointed him to a stick of wood. Moses threw it into the water and the water turned sweet. That's the place where God set up rules and procedures; that's where he started testing them. God said, "If you listen, listen obediently to how God tells you to live in His presence, obeying his commandments and keeping all His laws, then I won't strike you with all the diseases that I inflicted on the Egyptians; I am God your healer." (*Exodus 15:20-26)

These Scriptures describe the Israelites' gratitude when God performed a miracle of such great magnitude (parting The Red Sea). *Can you imagine witnessing such an event? Wow*!

They sang songs and worshipped God, and rightfully so. Just three days later, their praises turned to grumbling curses: "This desert sucks! Our travel guide Moses doesn't even know where he's going. We want some clean water to drink!"

Moses put up with a lot of complaining from the unfaithful, untrusting Israelites, but he kept trusting God. Moses prayed, thinking that maybe God would perform another awesome miracle to provide them with clean drinking water. Instead, God led Moses to a very ordinary solution. "Hey Mo, see that stick at your feet? Pick it up and throw it in the water." That's often how it goes with our "impossible" problems. The answer is often right in front of us, if we only stop and ask God to show us the answer.

God gave Moses clear, simple instructions to fix the bitter water problem. God tested Moses to see if he would listen and obey. This was one of many opportunities for Moses and the Israelites to live in God's glorious presence, even in the hot, dry wilderness. Despite their grumbling, God gave the Israelites a beautiful promise to protect them and heal them. But the promise was conditional: God expected them to listen and obey.

## Keys for Making Bitter Waters Sweet

Let's apply this story to our journey into and through the Wilderness of recovery. As we find ourselves standing in front of bitter waters, we must be very careful not to get ambushed by real feelings of abandonment, frustration, failure, fear, regret or hopelessness. You don't have to let your emotions rule your life.

As we walk through this leg of our journey, let's remember our backpack of tools. A construction worker doesn't go to the job site without one. God is helping you rebuild your life right now, and you can't afford to forget your tools, either. He wants to tear down things that have been built on a faulty foundation. He wants to straighten crooked walls and remove rotten boards. His architectural plans for you include "plans for peace and not disaster, plans for a future filled with hope." (Jeremiah 29:11) He is the perfect builder. He will help you reconstruct a life that will be whole, beautiful, healthy, and strong. But you have to be willing to cooperate with Him in the process – to listen and obey, just as He commanded the Israelites. He has provided all you need. If you prayed the prayer in the previous chapter, God sent His Holy Spirit to live inside of you. He will put ideas in your mind and peace in your heart that will lead you into the Promised Land. "*My sheep know my voice.*"(John 10:27)

Be careful not to think that Bible or book reading or superhuman spiritual discipline is the answer to your problems. This journey is more about your relationship with Jesus than it is about achievement. I recently prayed with a woman who wanted to know more of God's Word. The Lord's response to her was so beautiful. He let her know that she should first seek simply to *know Him better*. By first devoting herself to knowing Him better and understanding His nature and character, she would gain greater revelations from His Word.

We're tempted to think that merely memorizing words is the goal, or that our lives will be better if we study harder. Instead, let's press into a deep relationship with the Word-Giver. When we do, our times of study at His feet will be so much more alive. Two Greek words, *logos* and *rhema,* help us understand this principle. *Logos* represents the written Bible, and *rhema* represents a divine inner revelation from God, or the divinely breathed Word of God on a more personal level. We cannot expect to receive the *logos* if God's *rhema* isn't flowing through us.

## Practicing His Presence

In my introduction at speaking engagements, I often say I have a P.H.P. degree. That stands for *Practicing His Presence!* We could spend a lifetime earning degrees, certificates, and qualifications. But nothing is more important than sitting at the feet of Jesus, learning to love and serve Him; spending time talking to Him, and reading His word. He will become so real to you!

 As you grow in your relationship with the Lord, you will mature in spiritual disciplines because you'll have a growing desire to experience more. But the disciplines of praying, reading and meditating on God's Word, and fasting are not things you have to do perfectly. . Are you practicing His presence? I hope and pray that you can learn to praise Him in all things. It's simple to live a lifestyle of continual worship. Meditate on His Words. Strive to obey Him, and watch things change.

The Bible tells us that anointing breaks the yoke. (See Isaiah 10:27.) It helps us to practice remaining in the anointing.

In biblical days, a yoke was an apparatus that was placed around the neck and shoulders of an ox. An ox is a very strong and powerful animal, not easily controlled. The yoke is very hard and unyielding; it puts strict limits on the movement of the ox. The ox can't even move its head from side to side; it is forced to look straight forward. In the same way, sin, addictions, and wrong mindsets constrict our movement and thinking.

The anointing represents the unstoppable power of Christ. The more time we spend practicing His presence, the stronger the anointing (power of God). God's power breaks the yoke and sets us free.

The anointing comes as we remain in His presence. The more we worship, meditate, and obey God's word, (exercise our spirits) the stronger the anointing. Again, the word here is *practice*, so don't beat yourself up if you haven't figured out this principle.

I love this verse:

*You've been raised on the Message of the faith and have followed sound teaching. Now pass on this counsel to the followers of Jesus there, and you'll be a good servant of Jesus. Stay clear of silly stories that get dressed up as religion. Exercise daily in God—no spiritual flabbiness, please! Workouts in the gymnasium are useful, but a disciplined life in God is far more so, making you fit both today and forever. You can count on this. Take it to heart. This is why we've thrown ourselves into this venture so totally. We're banking on the living God, Savior of all men and women, especially believers. (*1 Timothy 4:6, MSG*)*

Now, let's break down a few concepts that the Israelites and your friends who have journeyed before you have learned along the way. Walking through the Wilderness can be extremely difficult if you don't understand the things that have caused you to wander and get frustrated. Some have even missed the Promised Land because they couldn't grasp these concepts. I pray that these insights will help you understand why you might still be wandering.

## Look for the Answer in the Question

Musician Michael Card said, "Could it be that questions tell us more than answers ever do?"[1]

That's a remarkable insight, and an especially important one when you think about all of the unanswered "whys" in your life. Perhaps we should not be so disappointed that the answer is hard to find. Perhaps Jesus wants to meet us in our quiet place of asking.

Rainer Maria Rilke said it like this: "I want to beg you to be patient toward all that is unsolved in your heart and try to love the questions themselves like locked rooms and like books that are written in a very foreign tongue. Do not seek the answers, which cannot be given you because you would not be able to live them. And the point is to live everything. Live the questions now. Perhaps you will then, gradually and without noticing it, live along some distant day into the answer."[2]

When I sat on my garage floor and shouted *"why?"* at God, I challenged Him to reveal why every horrific thing had happened to me. As I lived the question through the following months, I began to walk into the answers. Clarity increased as I got

---

1 Michael Card, *Present Reality/Joy in the Journey*, (Brentwood, TN: EMI/CMG Distribution, 2008).

2 Rainer Maria Rilke, Franz Xaver Kappus, and Reginald Snell, *Letters to a Young Poet* (Chemsford, MA: Courier Dover Publications, 2002).

involved in prison ministry. As I looked into every incarcerated woman's eyes, I was able to say and see that they were all part of my "Why." Not one of us asks "Why?" alone.

*Walk by faith and not by sight. (*2 Corinthians 5:7*)*

*Trust in the Lord with ALL your heart and do not rely on your own understanding. In ALL Your ways acknowledge Him and He will make your paths smooth. (*Proverbs 3:4-5, emphasis added*)*

Here is the answer to all of our questions! Jesus loves us. He has plans to prosper us and not to harm us. No matter the situation, He has a plan. *He's got it—all of it!*

*You hem me in--behind and before; you have laid your hand upon me. Such knowledge is too wonderful for me, too lofty for me to attain. (*Psalms 139:5-6*)*

Don't try to figure it out – walk it out. Don't wish it were different – we don't need "wishbones" as much as we need "backbones." We must not grow weary in doing what is right.

*It is for freedom that Christ has set us free. Stand firm, then, and do not let yourselves be burdened again by a yoke of slavery. (*Galatians 5:1*)*

*Arise, shine, for your light has come, and the glory of the Lord rises upon you. See, the darkness covers the earth and thick darkness is over the peoples, BUT the Lord rises upon you and His glory appears over you. (*Isaiah 60:1-2, emphasis added*)*

One key to getting out of the Wilderness is to take the trip without feeling like you have to have all the answers first. God told the Israelites they were going to a place flowing with milk and honey. Did they have some questions about this promise? You bet! The questions and the doubts struck them again and again. They doubted God's provision. They grumbled against the plan because they didn't understand, and they disobeyed.

If you are grumbling against God today, then my loving advice for you is to *cut it out!* Get with the program–*His* program! Choose to believe by faith that God knows exactly what He's doing. Line your thoughts and actions up to His plan; even if you see it as clearly as mud. Sooner or later, we'll all see it His way, so it's better to see it His way sooner.

That's enough for now. We'll talk about more helpful concepts for walking through the Wilderness in the next chapter.

## Stop And Think!

What are you bitter about? How has this bitterness negatively impacted your life?

_____

_____

_____

_____

What have you been grumbling and complaining about?

_____

_____

_____

_____

How have you thought you knew better than God?

_____

_____

_____

_____

How can you begin to turn more areas of your life over to God and trust Him more?

_____

_____

_____

_____

_____

What are your biggest gripes against God because you just don't understand something?

_____

_____

_____

_____

Can you keep trusting God and believe that He is good–that His plans for you are good–even if you don't understand?

_____

_____

_____

_____

_____

## Prayer Point

God, please help me to believe what I have yet to see! Please help me turn down the volume on my doubter! Just because I have a negative thought doesn't mean that I agree with it. Please help me control my thoughts and what comes out of my mouth. Please help me to walk with You, even when I cannot see where we are going. Forgive me for trying to go backwards.

When my thoughts tell me that I cannot trust You, I will say with my mouth, that I do trust You. *I trust you, Lord! I am ready to move forward!* Amen.

# Moving Forward, Not Backward
## Part 2.2

*Brothers, I do not consider myself yet to have taken hold of it. But one thing I do: Forgetting what is behind and straining toward what is ahead, I press on toward the goal to win the prize for which God has called me heavenward in Christ Jesus.* (Philippians 3:13-14)

Fear doesn't have power unless we give it authority. We empower fear when we fall prey to its lies. The Israelites were headed toward a wonderful destiny in the Promised Land. Unfortunately, they chose to embrace their fears rather than stand on and believe God's promises.

God had a perfect plan for them. All they had to do was stick to it. But life's not always that easy, is it? How many of us have stuck to God's plan? I know I sure haven't – not always. In fact, probably more often than not, I have wandered from the plan. The good thing is that the choice is getting easier as I get closer to Jesus. But sometimes, it takes a lot of milk and honey to wash the taste of the desert out of our mouths.

God's gifts are so much more excellent than the things of the desert. Just listen to His plans for the Israelites:

> *I have come down to rescue them from the hand of the Egyptians and to bring them up out of the land into a good and spacious land, a land flowing with milk and honey ....See, I am sending an angel ahead of you to guard you along the way and to bring you to the place I have prepared.* (Exodus 3:8, 23:20)

Now remember, God is the same yesterday, today, and forever. If you have asked for His help, He already has dispatched an angel to guard you along the way! He already has a place prepared for you! But if you continue to side with the enemy by allowing fear and unbelief into your heart, that angel is going to have to fight the powers of hell every step of the way! Your choices will affect how long and rough the journey will be.

## Relapse Mentality

Once the Israelites empowered their fear and focused on their circumstances instead of God's promise, another putrid thing happened. This is where the rubber met the road. I mean, this is where the sand met the sandal! They developed a "relapse mentality." They actually thought that going back into slavery in Egypt would be better than walking into God's promised destiny! They grumbled and complained. And even worse, they doubted God and questioned their leader, Moses.

These are some slippery places to walk on, my friend! If we're not careful, this type of thinking and speaking will lead us down bumpy, isolated, dead-end roads every time. It's a recipe for relapse!

> *Why is the Lord bringing us to this land only to let us fall by the sword? Our wives and children will be taken as plunder.* ***Wouldn't it be better for us to go back to Egypt?*** *(*Numbers 14:3, emphasis added*)*

Put your own personal "Egypt" at the end of that verse: "Wouldn't it be better to go back to the boyfriend who beats me? Wouldn't it be better to go back to prostitution, exotic dancing, stealing, or dealing drugs? At least then, I made a decent living. Wouldn't it be better to go back to using and drinking? At least then, I didn't feel so bad. Wouldn't it be better to go back to sleeping with him? At least then, I wasn't so lonely." Those were a few of my own thoughts, just to help you identify your own.

## The Journey Backwards Leads to Death

Here's an important point: relapse mentality leads to death. Every adult Israelite with those thoughts died in the wilderness. They actually forfeited the Promised Land because they preferred the stinking thinking of the wilderness. God planned to give them rich promises, but instead they received the poverty and death they spoke over themselves by grumbling and complaining. Let's see how this sad story continues:

> *"As surely as I live," declares the Lord, "I will do to you the very things I heard you say; In this desert your bodies will fall – every one of you*

*twenty years old or more ... who has grumbled against me. Not one of you will enter the land I swore with uplifted hand to make your home, except Caleb son of Jephunneh and Joshua son of Nun. As for your children that you said would be taken as plunder, I will bring them in to enjoy the land you have rejected ... Your children will be shepherds here for forty years, suffering for your unfaithfulness, until the last of your bodies lies in the desert."(*Numbers 14:28-33*)*

That seems like a harsh verdict. But remember, it's not what God had planned for them. His plan was Promised Land living. Not only did they talk their way right out of their destiny, but their poor children had to wander for *forty years*. It brings me to tears when I think about the years of wandering my children endured, and still might face, if I don't get a grip on the things I speak.

Hold onto this concept with all your might: you have the power of life and death in your tongue. Will you speak life or death? I pray that you will make a pact today to not let any "corrupt words come forth; except that which is edifying and uplifting." (Ephesians 4:29)

Reading the following verse should settle this right issue right now. God's Word puts heaven into action. Corrupt words put hell into action.

It only takes a spark to set a forest fire. A careless or wrongly placed word can ruin the world, turn harmony to chaos, throw mud on a reputation, send the whole world up in smoke, right from the pit of hell. (James 3:5-6, MSG)

God's Word is alive! Words originate with our thoughts. Words are spiritual containers that hold good or bad seeds that will grow.

## Wishy-Washy Thinking

Fear is a funny thing. Not funny as in "ha-ha," either. Fear and doubt cause us to lose sight of what God said. Remember how the devil deceived Eve in the garden? He asked her that little question, "Did your Father really say ...?" If we tiptoe and dance around doubt and fear, our whole world starts to shake. Maybe that's what James meant when he wrote:

*But when he asks, he must believe and not doubt, because he who doubts is like a wave of the sea, blown and tossed by the wind. That man should not think he will receive anything from the Lord, he is a double-minded man, unstable in all he does. (*James 1:6-8*)*

Wishy-washy thinking reflects our attitude toward God. One minute, we tell Him that we trust Him with our life. The next minute, we're turning our back on Him in worry and fear, not believing He cares about our problems. This is what the battle looks like!

We often muddle along, thinking we can handle all the lightweight stuff ourselves. In the Wilderness, we tend to cry out to God when we've gotten ourselves into a big mess; when we are desperate and need a miracle. Even worse; we blame Him for situations we create, or we accuse Him of having a fickle nature. This is not Promised Land living.

Do you ever think you know better than God? Have you ever thought He was crazy for having you do things that don't make sense to you? I have. Once, He wanted me to give someone some money. I knew that this person was still using drugs, and so my self-righteous attitude told me not to do it. I didn't want to cast my pearls to swine. Granted, there are times when we are not to take what is holy and feed it to the dogs. (Matthew 7:6) But that wasn't the case in this situation. God was prompting me specifically to bless this person, but I argued with Him. I told God. "No." I would not bless this person. Later, I learned more about the situation and it began to make sense to me. I felt horrible for not meeting such a small need that was well within my ability. Who did I think I was to say "No" to God? I thought I was pretty hot stuff to think I knew better than He.

*We know that we all possess knowledge. Knowledge puffs up, but love builds up. The man who thinks he knows something does not yet know as he ought to know. But the man who loves God is known by God. (*1 Corinthians 8:1-3*)*

## Every Day a Family Reunion

Being aware of dysfunctional family patterns can help us get through the Wilderness.

Have you ever attended your family reunion? Have you noticed how many different personality types are represented there? You see Aunt Ruth, who never sees the good in anyone. She squawks, complains, and gossips about the horrible things everyone else does. Did you ever hear her say she needs to work on seeing the good in people? Probably not.

How about Uncle Tom? Isn't he a pervert? He always cracks sexually offensive jokes. He tells all the nieces and cousins to give him kisses and hugs. He offers constant invitations to sit on his lap so he can tell you something funny. Maybe you've always even been his VERY favorite. The rest of the family just says that's his way of showing affection. It just doesn't seem right.

Then there's Mom. Boy, she will do and do and do for people. Not in a good way, either. She always seems miserable. She just can't seem to say "No." But under the "Yes" is resentment that she always reminds you about. She tells you how nobody else does anything for themselves … that she's always the one to do it if it's going to get done….that if it weren't for her, the family wouldn't survive.

Then there's Dad. Where is he, anyway? You can see his body, but his mind is always somewhere else. He's detached, unavailable, silent, missing in action.

This was my family. This is how I grew up. I thought my family was normal; that everyone's family looked just like mine. Of course, all of our problems stayed within the family. Nobody had to know about Aunt-So-and-So and Uncle-You-Know-Who. That was just between us. Your family may not look like mine. It's not *exactly* what mine looks like, either. But you get the point. Until we understand our family dynamics through self-examination, most of us live at a family reunion, where we just accept dysfunction as the truth.

Have you ever heard the expression: "Hurt people—hurt people?" We bring into adulthood the experiences and knowledge we gained as children. We record what we learn from those around us. We play recordings of our influential role models over and over again, and these people's personalities influence how we relate to others. They influence how we see ourselves and the world around us. Is the world a good place? Is it a safe place? Do I matter? Does my opinion count? Am I worthy of good things? Is there such a thing as forgiveness, mercy, and grace? Am I surrounded by beauty? Where can I place my hope and trust? These questions, and many others, are answered during our childhood.

## Shame that Binds and Blinds

I shared with you earlier that from the age of three, I performed in pageants. Performance and perfectionism became the measure of my worth, both on stage and off. The world became my judge, and anything less than perfect marks left me feeling shameful and worthless. It didn't matter where I was or whom I was with; I was living for applause and affirmation. I felt like a pile of trash under my judges' feet.

Since then, I have realized the huge difference between excellence and perfectionism. A spirit of excellence leads me to do everything to the best of my ability. On the other hand, perfectionism tells me that no matter how well I do something, it

still isn't good enough. It could have been better, if only I'd have….whatever. I beat myself up and waste precious time, energy, and emotion trying to achieve better than my best. And my best may change from one day to the next. The height of the bar always changes, and usually it goes up.

Have you ever felt like you were the only caterpillar in a butterfly world? Do you often feel as if you have to do twice as much to be half as good as others?

Author Sandra D. Wilson calls these feelings "binding shame."[1] She writes that, "Shame is rooted in the lie that human beings can and should be perfect. And yet I know I am imperfect. And because I know I'm not perfect, I view myself as hideously flawed. So when I make a mistake, I don't simply make a mistake: I believe I *am* a mistake.

That is shame's lie in a nutshell. And that lie becomes the lens through which we see every experience. When I am bound by shame, it contaminates all my perceptions, choices, and relationships. What's more, a shameful self-perspective leaves me feeling isolated from everyone else. I believe that my only chance to connect with perfect people is either to convince them that I can fill a need in their life or to trick them into thinking that I too am perfect."

Shame not only binds us; it blinds us. It makes it nearly impossible to honestly examine ourselves. Yet on our journey through the Wilderness of recovery, this is exactly what we must do. We need honest self-examination before we can have a deep, lasting, redemptive experience.

## Moving Forward in Honest Self-Examination

Having a knock-down, bang-up crisis moment–like mine, among the broken shards of my glass pipe many years ago–makes honest self-examination easier. When your life is a mess and everybody knows it, the gig is up. What more is there to hide?

Some say that being aware of your faults is half the battle. If that's true, then the awareness is the easy half. When you become aware of your faults, you also become accountable to do something about them. This second part of the process is what it means to walk through the Wilderness; to put on your sandals and travel–step-by-step-by-step–through the dusty landscape. That takes a lot more determination.

As we move forward, there comes a time to examine everything intensely. Once again, we confront the questions: "What are my choices? Which way do I want to go;

---

1 Sandra D. Wilson, *Hurt People Hurt People* (Grand Rapids, MI: Discovery House Publishers, 2001).

backward or forward? Do I want to hurt people all my life? How long can I live with this insanity? Why do I act this way, anyway? Why do I think like this? Why can't I stop saying mean things? Why do I live under such shame and condemnation?"

Without this examination process, these questions remain unanswered. It has been said that "If nothing changes; nothing changes." It seems life-threatening to see and acknowledge our imperfections. That's why we close our eyes to them. We are afraid to risk honest self-examination to find integrity and wholeness. But ignoring a problem never helps. The problem only gets worse!

You can't heal a wound by pretending it isn't there. To do so wouldn't be honest, and God places a high value on truth. Jesus called Himself the Truth. (John 14:6) If we're not careful, lies will become a distorted, tainted lens through which we see every experience and every relationship, including our relationship with God. Instead of a merciful Father who is leading us to a beautiful land flowing with milk and honey, we see a "god" who beats us down, laughs at us, and calls us inadequate and unworthy. If only we could fathom the enormous height, breadth, and depth of His unconditional love for us!

*And I pray that you, being rooted and established in love, may have power, together with all the saints, to grasp how wide and long and high and deep is the love of Christ. (*Ephesians 3:18, NIV*)*

In our journey through the Wilderness, God insists that we get to know Him as He really is. He wants us to allow Him to be Himself, not some caricature of a "god" we see through our defective lens of personal experiences.

Will God endorse or anoint a counterfeit? Will God give His stamp of approval on your life of denial? He wouldn't do it for me. While we may think that we are getting away with something by living with our eyes closed to the truth about ourselves, God focuses on our unseen, inner lives. This is what Scripture calls our "heart." Proverbs 4:23 tells us to "watch over" or "guard" our heart because our words and actions flow out of our unseen, inner lives. God is unlikely to give us wisdom when we keep ignoring the "hidden stuff."

> *Whoever covers over his sins does not prosper. Whoever confesses and abandons them receives compassion.(* Proverbs 28:13*)*

When we hide from painful truths, we deprive ourselves of the discovery that Jesus, the Great Physician, is able to heal our emotional wounds, just as surely as He is able to forgive our sins.

## Stop And Think!

What situations cause you the most fear?

_____

_____

_____

_____

_____

How have you given authority to fear instead of to God? How can you change that, starting today?

_____

_____

_____

_____

_____

Are you tempted to believe that things were better back in Egypt? Imagine life back there, with all the fighting, addictions, and junk. How can you refute Satan's lie that things were better then?

_____

_____

_____

_____

_____

Describe your feelings about your family's dysfunctions. What can you work on to change an area of this dysfunction?

_____

_____

_____

_____

_____

Are you ready to honestly examine yourself, warts and all? Secondly, are you ready to accept the fact that Jesus loves you with infinite love, and that you can't do anything to earn His love?

_____

_____

_____

_____

_____

In what ways have you grown since you began this journey through the wilderness?

_____

_____

_____

_____

_____

What lies has God revealed to you? What is the truth of God in comparison to those lies?

_____

_____

_____

_____

_____

## Prayer Point

God, I confess that I haven't trusted You. There have been times when I have blatantly disobeyed You. I ask for your forgiveness. I realize that I cannot take this journey through the Wilderness without fully relying on You. I do not want to wander here. I want to be purposeful about getting through to the Promised Land. Please help me to lean on You and not on my own understanding.

Father, give me the courage to examine my ways and test them. Holy Spirit, please reveal the areas of dysfunction that have operated in my family for generations. God, with Your power and my willingness to work through the Wilderness, I pray that my children will get to enjoy the Promised Land also. Help me to keep my mind fixed on You.

Lord, I do not want to continue to be a hurt person who hurts other people. Please help me to see the relationships in my life through Your lens. Father, if there are relationships that I will have to walk away from in this journey, please help me to do that. Your grace is sufficient. You have invited me to stand up from the midst of my sinful acts like the adulterous woman in John 8. Your words to me are the same as Your words to her: "Go and sin no more." Help me to accomplish this Father, so that I can experience Promised Land living.

Help me, Lord, to keep a careful watch over my mouth. Moreover, let the meditations of my heart be pleasing in Your sight. Transform me inside and out as I walk through the Wilderness. I trust wholeheartedly in your plan to usher me into the Promised Land.

In Jesus' Name, Amen!

# Pitch a Tent, Not Build a House
## Part 2.3

### Is This it, God?

Yes, it's true that God had the Israelites take the journey through the wilderness the long way. But remember, even that long way could have taken days – not years. Our recovery process may be necessary for our training and entrance into the Promised Land. I don't know exactly what your recovery experience will look like. It may involve a residential program. It could take a few years of meetings, support, sponsorship, and steps. It could take intensive counseling.

If God has brought you this far, He will provide. It is His nature to give you everything you need to make it through this season. For the Israelites, He provided a cloud by day, fire by night, manna each morning, and clothes and shoes that didn't wear out. As you take your journey through the Wilderness, you may need to be emotionally prepared to pitch a tent and camp for a little while. The process of your brokenness didn't happen overnight, and your journey into wholeness may not, either. It likely will take time and effort to retrain the way you think, act, speak, and walk through life. But while you are camped out here, don't anticipate or set your mind to take up permanent residence. Don't make curtains for your pit. Build a ladder out. Carve a window to see through to the other side. Don't lose sight that your current condition is not where you will spend the remainder of your days.

I clearly remember sitting in the recovery rooms and thinking, *If this is how I am going to have to spend the rest of my life, I'm just not sure I'm willing to do it. I mean, is this all there is to look forward to?* I came in feeling like I had already wasted a decade of my life. I didn't want my hope to be limited to what I saw and experienced in a recovery program! I firmly set my mind to the process and determined that I wouldn't merely settle for sobriety – I was going for all-out recovery! I wasn't even aware that my yearning desire was biblical, because my knowledge of the Word was limited.

I had no idea at the time that Jesus Christ died on the cross so that I could live in abundance, and that abundance was what I yearned for.

Sometimes, when I have the opportunity to speak to an audience, I jokingly misquote the Bible verse to say that "Jesus said that He died so that we might have life and have it more redundantly." Then, I pause and wait for the response. No, that *isn't* what Jesus said He died for. No wonder I was unsettled in my spirit about the possibility of having to build a house, take up residence, and remain in the rooms of recovery for the rest of my life. To do so would be the equivalent of wandering and dying in the Wilderness.

After completing a recovery process, one of my dear friends shared this written piece with me. She gladly allowed me to include it here, to be a blessing to you. Here is what she was feeling at the time:

*I have almost completed something that has changed my life.*

*I do not want to stay in this hospital that has set all my broken pieces in place, going over and over all the same wounds. Yet where do I go? Where do I step out to ... when I leave the safety of my group?*

*I am uncomfortable starting a new group. I do not want to open up to anyone new. I do not want to surf shallow waters, nor dig up something I just buried.*

*I feel like I'm still very vulnerable and defensive. It is not that women are my enemy. But not all of them are digging nor have dug as deeply as I have recently. I feel carved; like a ritual has been performed on me. And I am now part of a tribe that is very distinct. I have been marked. Not that I am so special.*

*But some things have been taken out. And I must be very careful what goes in. This is tender skin and tissue. I don't want foreign matter falling in. ....just because I am still open and vulnerable.*

*The surgery has taken place. The bones are set. But this is a time of knitting....it is very, very crucial. I do not want to let any unwholesome thing invade this place of healing.*

*I feel like I'm in the final stages of a cocoon. No tapping. No meddling allowed. This is a holy, sacred thing. I feel like pulling away from, yet I am being drawn towards, that which is still not visible. The egg is not hatched, but will be any time now. And so I must watch over this small thing and guard it--though I do not know what it is or what it will become.*

*What I must nourish it with is new. I am unfamiliar with this food. I am groping for something I do not know.*

*My Master, on the other hand, has slipped His hand in mine and said, "Come. Come away with Me." He placed His fingers on my lips and said, "Do not speak." I am not used to this command. "Be still and know that I am God."*

*I want to run away. But He says, "Run away to me. I will seal your wounds in My balm. I will close the openings and the doors you cannot. I will search out and seize any harmful micro-organisms that have wreaked havoc in your body, soul, and spirit. I am your healer. I am your therapist. I am interested in your ongoing recovery. I have totally covered you. Come away with Me in the Secret Place. Cease all activity. Quiet. Be quiet. Do not tamper with this process. I am the author and the finisher. Trust Me."*

*Kitty Lyon, March 2008*

No one can define what your personal recovery (journey through the Wilderness) will look like. We all have different experiences. But we know that if we serve the same God, and the promises and plans in His Word apply to us, they can apply to anyone. My beliefs have changed drastically from the first day I stepped into the rooms of recovery. I hope to expand your vision for recovery to include the hope of absolute freedom! I have talked with fellow friends in recovery about whether or not we still claim to be addicts/alcoholics, or say that we are in recovery. I choose to believe and state publicly that I am saved, redeemed, and recovered. Why? Because there is power in the words we confess.

*I refuse to proclaim that I struggle with a former identity that Christ has washed clean!*

God said that if we abide in Him, He will abide in us. We can build our home in His presence. On this promise, I choose to hang my hat and hope.

For a season, the groups, the sponsors, and the steps were our higher power. But it didn't take God long to let me know that He is a jealous God, and that I should not be ashamed of the gospel that set me free. Nothing could compare to the blood of Jesus that washed me clean. I was not to give credit, glory or power to anyone or anything else. My willingness to acknowledge the true source of my power and recovery can indicate whether or not I have pitched a tent in the Wilderness or have moved on to build a house. Do we plan to live in this space forever, or are we simply passing through?

When you find yourself getting discouraged and thinking that things won't get better, please read the following verse. After you read it, write it down and put it somewhere for instant access. I hope it blesses and encourages you, as it has me:

*And this small and temporary trouble we suffer will bring us a tremendous and eternal glory, much greater than the trouble. (*2 Corinthians 4:17*)*

The Bible also tells us that this life on earth, compared to the eternity we will spend in heaven, is a mere vapor. It is a very short time! So, no matter how long our journey through the Wilderness is, we know it won't be forever. Keep going; it doesn't always have to be this way. The Promised Land is right on the other side of the mountain.

## Stop And Think!

How does it feel to believe you actually could step into the Promised Land?

_____

_____

_____

_____

_____

How has this concept of the Promised Land changed the way you think about your recovery process?

_____

_____

_____

_____

_____

How can you speed up your journey through the Wilderness?

_____

_____

_____

_____

_____

Do you believe you were destined for the Promised Land? Why or why not?

_____

_____

_____

_____

_____

Describe your feelings about the possibility of a new horizon. How long has it been since you've dared to dream of a different life?

_____

_____

_____

_____

_____

## Prayer Point

 God, I confess that I have bought into the lie that this process could be too difficult; that it could take the rest of my life. Lord, I know that You said I can do all things through You. I want to have a vision for myself in the Promised Land. I want to believe that I won't spend the rest of my life just struggling to get by. Lord, even in my belief, help my unbelief. Help me to remember that You have a plan for my life that doesn't include wandering until I die in the Wilderness. Give me Your eyes, God, that I might see my life as You see it. Help me to remember that You will give me beauty for the ashes of my past. Please help me to trust that You will make all things new as I surrender my past, present, and future to You. In Jesus' name, Amen.

# Transition Time
## Coming Out Of The Wilderness

Hey, dude!

It has been so long since I've writen. You probably thought I was dead. (Ha, ha.) I could fill a library with my stories about this dry and crusty desert. But here's the good news – we're moving out of here tomorrow! Happy days are soon to come.

Things are looking up!

P.S. As usual, I've attached a few photos.

## Snapshots of Leaving the Wilderness

Hi, I'm Deanna.

I thank God for my recovery in the Wilderness, and I praise Him for the good people who helped me through it. A great moment of revelation came when I learned that I didn't have to remain in recovery forever. When I look back over my seven years in recovery, I'd guess that I spent one thousand hours in meetings alone. By the end of that time, I felt like a trapped bird. I was screaming for fresh air and freedom. I hadn't come this far to die in the Wilderness.

I discovered that if you are not careful, recovery itself can become an addiction. I discovered that the same internal force that chained me to drugs and alcohol could chain me to my recovery meetings. My peers told me I must remain in the Wilderness of recovery for the rest of my life. It was so sad to see how many of them had been victorious over their addictions, but now were living in total defeat. Their marriages were falling apart and their lives were in shambles. They had simply replaced a substance addiction with a meeting addiction. Week after week, I heard the same old stories over and over again. They definitely were not living the victorious life Jesus had promised – but neither was I!

I went round and round a crazy hamster wheel of recovery meetings, hoping that there was more to life. It wasn't easy on my husband and kids, who were bearing the burden of all these meetings and my defeatist attitude. Thankfully, a quiet voice in my heart was telling me that a beautiful, peaceful life awaited me just across the Jordan River. I only had to cross over to find it. And that little voice grew stronger and stronger each day.

I finally made up my mind. I decided to skip the meetings and go on a family vacation. Sure, I felt a little insecure. Those old, familiar voices in my head were telling me I was going to fail. But God's voice was telling me it was time to go and that I would be all right, as long as I held tightly to Him and remembered His promises.

I left the recovery rooms and God was faithful. He was waiting to receive me in the Promised Land, and it was much better than I even imagined.

*Hi, I'm Michelle.*

*Anyone who has been in a recovery room–either Christian or secular–has heard the same thing: "Keep coming back. You will need recovery for the rest of your life. If you don't come to meetings, you will have a relapse–guaranteed."*

*I had heard those things since I was a young child. My whole family struggles with alcoholism, drug addiction, dysfunctional relationships–the list goes on and on. From the time I was 10 years old, I went to meetings with family members. I heard stories about people who had been going for twenty years or more. They told me that since my dad was an alcoholic, I'd be an alcoholic too, and I'd have to live my life in recovery. It's like having a self-fulfilling curse spoken over your life! I have had addiction spoken over me since I was a little girl, over and over, until it was ingrained in my spirit.*

*Then I started going to church, where I heard things like "You are a new creation in Christ! You can be delivered by the power of God! You are free!" That's when my two worlds collided and I didn't know how to resolve the conflict. After several years in both church and recovery meetings, I just gave up. I believed the lie that God wasn't big enough to heal me like He had healed other people. I went to recovery meetings and felt like they were lying to me because it contradicted what I heard from my pastors. I played the game, acting like I was fine at church, but inside, I wanted to die. Every day, I just wanted to die.*

*Thankfully, God led me to enroll in a Christian program for women with serious life-controlling issues. I went in with a long list of identifying issues: I called myself a cutter, an alcoholic, an addict, and an abused girl. I never thought of myself as anything more than damaged goods. This program taught me things that were hard to believe at first: You will not always* struggle with this. You are not an alcoholic. You are not a drug addict. You are not a used, tainted girl from sexual abuse. You have a choice in picking up your addictions, or in saying "No" to them, with God's help.

I was amazed! I'd had this lifelong word-curse spoken over me. I believed I could never change, and these people told me that I can be free and no longer struggle with these issues. I thought they were off their rockers! God told me to trust Him when I went there, but was He crazy? Was this some kind of a cult?

I'm happy to say that God began to heal me through that program, and as He did, my trust increased. For the first time ever, I believed that this powerful Scripture applied to me: "He whom the Son sets free is free indeed." (John 8:36) So, I got bold and started saying "No" to my flesh when I wanted to self-injure or give in to my addictions. And the more I refused, the easier it got.

I was not able to do this with my own strength, but with God's strength. The people who told me I would never be able to control my addictions were actually right about that. But they didn't know how strong and loving God is. He alone is able to control our addictions.

I'm proud to say that today God has shown me I don't have to be ruled by my past. My addictions are not a part of me anymore. They are nailed to the cross, crucified with Jesus, allowing me to rise above the curses that were spoken over me. It wasn't easy crushing the twenty-seven-year mindset of "you will always need recovery." Finding freedom was a difficult process. But God is always faithful and His Word will never be spoken without causing good things to happen. The Truth will always conquer the darkness and I'm proud to say that my addictions and the Wilderness of recovery are now behind me.

*Hi, I'm Cris.*

*Recovery meetings helped me a lot, up to a point. Then, after about a year, I knew I had to go on with my life beyond recovery. My relationship with Jesus was growing incredibly and He was saying that He wanted me to share the things I had learned with others. He wanted my identity to change so that people would not just see me as a recovering addict or an ex-user, but as a fully recovered and redeemed child of God.*

*Some people didn't understand my decision. They said that I was nailing my coffin shut if I stopped going to recovery meetings. But I had to obey God's voice. In fact, my transition out of the Wilderness of recovery was all about getting to know God on a more intimate level. He was saying, "You've been to enough meetings now. Don't run to a meeting. Run to My heart." That's also when I finally really fell in love with my husband for the first time in eleven years, and when I learned to cherish my children like never before. I was applying the tools I'd learned to use and falling in love with my family.*

*It wasn't until I stepped away from the rooms of recovery that I fully recovered. But that recovery didn't happen because of my own strength. I'm learning to allow God to be strong in my weakness and brokenness. I was overcome with an intense yearning for everything that the Promised Land offered me spiritually, mentally, and physically. I didn't care what obstacles stood in my way. I didn't care how big the giants were. God promised me a beautiful inheritance in the land ahead, and I knew I could never be satisfied with anything less.*

Hi, I'm Troy.

The main thing you should know about my Wilderness experience is that I didn't want to be there. I would have much rather been doing drugs or drinking with all my snowboarding friends. I was on the verge of going to jail for a bad Driving Under the Influence (D.U.I.) accident. My parents came to my so-called "rescue" by offering to send me out of state to a rehab program. They said if I didn't go, they would kick me out of their house, where I'd been living. Basically, they were saying, "Go to rehab or go to jail."

"Wow," I thought. "This sucks. My parents hate me. I don't have a choice." I didn't think I needed rehabilitation, but it was all I could do to stay out of jail. So I went.

It was a really tough Christian program and I hated the loss of my freedom. The worst thing was all that 24/7 Jesus crap. It was driving me crazy and I wanted to go home. One day, we went to an obligatory church service led by a visiting preacher. He was an annoying guy who spoke with a Texas drawl. I was counting the minutes until we'd get out of there, when he said he wanted to pray for us.

He said, "There's someone here who is having problems with his hands. God wants to heal the pain. Come forward so that we can pray for healing."

A shiver went down my spine. My hands were hurting very badly. As a result of attending massage school, I had carpal tunnel; my hands had been hurting for months, but I was too cool to have people pray for me. As far as I was concerned, Christianity and healing was a hoax.

"Receive healing for your hands," the man urged. "Jesus wants to heal you." I could not believe it. There was no possible way this man could have known about my hands. He kept calling me forward, and finally, I gave in. I reluctantly went up to the front of the church.

A bunch of people started praying for me—and I mean praying really loudly. It all seemed so strange. Then suddenly, I blacked out. When I came to, it was so amazing—the pain was gone! Totally gone! I mean, my wrists were super inflamed all the time. I had these huge knots in and on them. I could hardly hold things without dropping them. And suddenly, I was completely healed! I had no explanation whatsoever, short of a miracle of God. I knew that God had answered those prayers.

That was the beginning of my swift journey not only out of Egypt, but also out of the Wilderness of recovery. I changed overnight into a total believer in Jesus. I began to care about rehab and I lost all desire for the things of the past. I made new Christian friends and God began to restore some of the family relationships I'd messed up in the past. I developed a passion to read the Bible and learn more about this incredible God. The awesome thing is that although I didn't care at all about God at the time, He loved me so much that He sought me out of Egypt and set me on the road to the Promised Land. What a great God!

Hi, I'm E.J.

I just can't do it anymore. I once believed that there was a place called the Promised Land, but now all I know are the chains of Egypt and this hopeless Wilderness. I haven't been able to find my way from one place to the other and I don't want either one of them. I'm tired of all this crap. I'm giving up the fight. This black cloud is killing me.

This is Deanna—and it's with tears in my eyes that I tell you that my little brother, E.J., didn't make it. He was found dead in his isolation cell in San Quentin on June 9, 2005. I sincerely believe that he wanted to reach the Promised Land with all his heart. He was getting a clearer picture of Egypt and he was seeing some great success in breaking free of its bondages. But for every step forward, he was beaten backward by the "system" and the consequences of bad choices he had spent a lifetime making. He'd go to rehab for a while and have some big victories, and then he'd fall back into Egypt when the pressures became too great.

His last journey out of Egypt and into the Wilderness was the longest ever. He was home and out of trouble for almost a year. He'd even started a business and gotten engaged. Then life came crashing down on him again, and he went back to prison. He saw himself as a grasshopper, compared to the giants that stood in his way. He died in a cloud of spiritual oppression and defeat. He missed out on the glorious rewards of walking into the Promised Land on this earth. Still, I hope to see him walking free and victorious in God's eternal kingdom some day. But I can't find the words to describe how much I miss my little brother, E.J., today.

The circumstances and causes of my brother's death are still clouded in confusion, and I don't want them to be a distraction to the message of this book. My hope and prayer for you is that you do not give up five minutes before your big breakthrough. You can be victorious, and I want to be the first one to welcome you (after Jesus) when you come into glory across that heavenly finish line. And remember, victorious living in the Promised Land is available to you here and now, not just in heaven some day.

# The Battle for the Other Side
## Part 2.4

My dad is retired now, but years ago, he drove a mountain mover. Actually, the correct term would be an "earth mover." If you've never seen earth moving equipment close-up and in- person, you don't know what you're missing. The tires themselves are massive. I stood inside one of them and I couldn't even reach from side to side with my arms spread wide. My dad climbed an extremely high ladder to reach his driver's seat. He was just a regular person like you and me, but with the strength of that monstrous machine, he could rip into dirt and rock like a spoon digging into whipped cream. In minutes, he'd move more tons of earth than you or I could hope to move by hand in a lifetime. I felt tiny in the shadow of that enormous equipment.

We all need a mountain mover in our lives. Do you ever feel small, compared to the massive mountains you face? I'm guessing that you do. Thankfully, our toolbox contains a mountain mover called faith.

> *If you have faith in God and don't doubt, you can tell this mountain to get up and jump into the sea, and it will. (*Mark 11:23, CEV*)*

## Rows of Little Box Houses

I was in an airplane recently, looking down on a city with its row of box-like houses. From so high up in the air, I realized that any one of those houses could have been mine.

> *Keep your minds fixed on things above, not on things here on earth.* (Colossians 3:2*)*

Sometimes, we look at situations in our lives with the same perspective. If we fix our mind on the spiritual things of God's kingdom above, everything earthly starts

to shrink and come into God's perspective. When I looked at those houses from an aerial view, every house looked the same size–miniscule. But if I stand directly in front of my house, it looks much, much larger. If I opened the front door and walked inside, I would be totally consumed by my house. It would be all around me. Everywhere I look, I would see nothing but house. In the same way, our problems look so huge when we fix our mind on them. If we aren't careful, we can become consumed by them. *But* if we look at our problems and situations with an aerial view (kingdom perspective) our problems look smaller, manageable, and more like everyone else's.

When we keep our mind fixed on things above, God helps us not to be consumed by the things on earth – no matter how big they seem! God encouraged me by showing me that at the end of my life, all of my problems will look small. I probably won't even be able to tell one from the other. Think of all the times you worried about not having enough money. I'll bet God provided for you and you didn't die of hunger. Or, what did you worry about five years ago?...ten years ago?....or fifteen? Eventually, all those problems will look like those little box houses I saw from 20,000 feet in the air.

God cares about your problems. He asks us not to worry about them, but rather to entrust them to Him. That's easier to do when you remember that He owns all the big mountain-moving equipment.

> *Then they cried to the Lord in their trouble, and He saved them out of their distresses. He sent His Word and healed them, and delivered them from their destruction. Oh, that men would give thanks to the Lord for His goodness, and for His wonderful works to the children of men. Let them sacrifice sacrifices of thanksgiving, and declare His works with rejoicing. (*Psalms 107:19-22)*

When we cry out to God, He saves us from our distresses. God is able and willing! By His Word, He heals us and delivers us from destruction. To keep a heavenly perspective on life, I find it extremely helpful to thank the Lord for His goodness and wonderful works in the midst of trials. It's easy to give thanks when times are good. But God wants us to fix our mind on Him and stand on His promises during the difficult times, too. If we fix our mind on the problems and the frustrations, it's like singing a song of praise to Satan. I'd rather sing praises to Jesus! Are we believers or are we not? If we truly believe, then why are we so consumed by our problems instead of standing in faith on the promises of God?

## Grasshoppers and Earth-Movers

So, where is your focus? On the mountain-like problems? On your feelings that make you seem small in comparison? Or on God's earth-moving equipment?

The story of the Israelites gives us a picture of God's mountain-moving power. The Israelites went through the wilderness, grumbling, complaining, and even worshipping idols. But God helped them, and finally, they arrived at the border of the Promised Land. This was their magic moment. They were standing on the threshold of this glorious destiny God had prepared for them. Here's what happed next:

> *The Lord said to Moses, "Choose one of the leaders from each of the twelve tribes and send them as spies to explore the land of Canaan, which I am giving to the Israelites." Moses obeyed and from the wilderness of Paran he sent out leaders ...* (Numbers 13:1-3)

Moses chose the well respected leaders of the twelve tribes of Israel. The story continues:

> *When Moses sent them out, he said to them, "Go north from here into the southern part of the land of Canaan and then on into the hill country. Find out what kind of country it is, how many people live there, and how strong they are. Find out whether the land is good or bad and whether the people live in open towns or in fortified cities. Find out whether the soil is fertile and whether the land is wooded. And be sure to bring back some of the fruit that grows there." (It was the season when grapes were beginning to ripen.)*(Numbers 13:17-20)

God asked Moses to conduct some research before moving into the Promised Land. This story reminds me of the many times God asked me to test the promises He had spoken over me. He would send me somewhere and say, "Just hang out with these people. See what they're like. Watch how they are living life and doing things. Just go, and then I'll instruct you about what to do next."

Here's what happened in the story of the Israelite spies:

> *So the men went north and explored the land ... They came to Eshcol Valley, and there they cut off a branch which had one bunch of grapes on it so heavy that it took two men to carry it on a pole between them. They also brought back some pomegranates and figs ... After exploring the land for forty days, the spies returned to Moses, Aaron, and the whole community*

*of Israel at Kadesh in the wilderness of Paran. They reported what they had seen and showed them the fruit they had brought. They told Moses, "We explored the land and found it to be rich and fertile; and here is some of its fruit. But...."* (Numbers 13:21-27)

The spies saw a rich and beautiful land. They even brought back some of the delicious fruit as evidence of its richness. Basically, they said, "God was right. This place is pretty darned good. The food is tasty and fresh, especially compared to our wilderness rations. We accomplished our mission in forty days. Been there, done that, bought the grapes. *But....*"

### Tune in Next Week–Same Time, Same Channel ...

This is cliff-hanger time. Let's pause a moment here and talk about our own journey, lest we forget that this story is about us, too. It's easy to read stories in the Bible and forget how much they apply to what is going on in our own lives. We're talking about our personal journey through the Wilderness to the Promised Land, right?

So, how many times have we said things like, "This time is going to be different. This time, I'm not falling back into that abusive, dysfunctional relationship. This time, I'm going to get my kids back and raise them right. This time, I'm staying clean (for more than ninety days). This time, I'm going to stay plugged into a church where I can grow and be fed. This time, I'm going to get and keep a good job. This time, I'm not going to say those mean and hurtful words."

These are a few "this times" from my own memory bank. Whatever your "this time" is, it's a glimpse of the Promised Land. It's a sneak preview of a victorious life. For a moment, we might even muster up enough faith to believe that we can experience some of the things we have spied out and watched other people do.

We take our little tour bus into the Promised Land so we can press our noses to the window and watch how people live there. We shoot pictures. We take plenty of notes in our travel diaries. We even jump off the bus to grab clumps of fruit. Then, the bus takes us back home and we show others our souvenirs and tell them what victorious life in the Promised Land is all about.

"It's a beautiful land," we say. "*But ...*"

# Big Buts

Personally, I don't believe in plastic surgery (although as gravity takes its toll on me and I develop new "features," I may change my stance on this). Nevertheless, I will add one note here for a little comic relief: *Big buts* (not "butts") don't have a place in the Promised Land.

The story continues:

> *They told Moses, "We explored the land and found it to be rich and fertile; and here is some of its fruit.* **BUT** *the people who live there are powerful, and their cities are very large and well fortified. Even worse, we saw the descendants of the giants there. Amalekites live in the southern part of the land; Hittites, Jebusites, and Amorites live in the hill country; and Canaanites live by the Mediterranean Sea and along the Jordan River."*
>
> *Caleb silenced the people who were complaining against Moses, and said, "We should attack now and take the land; we are strong enough to conquer it." But the men who had gone with Caleb said, "No, we are not strong enough to attack them; the people there are more powerful than we are." So they spread a false report among the Israelites about the land they had explored. They said, "That land doesn't even produce enough to feed the people who live there. Everyone we saw was very tall, and we even saw giants there, the descendants of Anak. We felt as small as grasshoppers, and that is how we must have looked to them." (*Numbers 13:27-33**,** emphasis added)*

Isn't this account just like our own lives? We make our way through the Wilderness believing that God has spoken Promised Land things into our heart. We even go check them out, grab some grapes, and tell a friend we scoped it out. *But,* when we start looking at ourselves, instead of keeping our eyes fixed on things above and trusting the One who sent us to get the promise, we start seeing ourselves as grasshoppers. We start seeing our challenges as giants. It's kind of like being swallowed by our house instead of looking down on it from the window of an airplane.

Achieving the things the Lord has put in our hearts may not come easy. Believe me, I know that there are many mountains to climb and giants to face. But do you see yourself as a grasshopper? Does it seem like things are just too difficult to manage? Do people have too much power over you and your life? Does it seem impossible to take possession of the land?

So many of us have felt this way. That's why it's crucial that you see yourself as God sees you. Even more importantly, you must see God for who *He is!* He is our mountain mover. There is nothing He cannot do. Even if we see Him as someone who twirls galaxies on His fingers and raises armies of dead men back to life, our view of Him is still tiny. He is bigger than bigger than big. Our most impossible obstacles are nothing to Him.

This view of God requires the kind of faith that we read about earlier, in Mark 11:23: "If you have faith….you can tell this mountain." Our progress doesn't depend on our own strength, but on God's, as we recognize our own weakness. In fact, the more we admit our weakness and inability to do anything good in our own strength, the stronger and more powerful God will become on our behalf. Don't fall into the trap of self-sufficiency, believing we are able to move mountains by our own strength. We must rely fully on God's strength.

We're like I was, as a little girl of seven, looking up to my father in that massive earth-moving equipment:

"Daddy, there's a big mountain in my way. Can you move it for me?"

"Sure thing, honey."

My father moves the mountain. When I get up and dust off my clothes, I can see into the Promised Land.

"Thanks, Daddy!"

## Stop And Think!

Are you facing giant mountains? How have you tried to move them in your own strength?

_____

_____

_____

_____

_____

What more have you learned about that you can turn over to God? How do you think He can take care of things that are too big for you to handle?

_____

_____

_____

_____

_____

How have "buts" caused you to doubt that God is able?

_____

_____

_____

_____

_____

In what ways have you been living as a grasshopper? What will help you remain strong?

_____

_____

_____

_____

_____

## Prayer Point

God, I have leaned on my own understanding and I've taken matters into my own hands for so long that it seems difficult to turn them over to You. And yet, there's something inside telling me it's okay; that I will be free. I'm looking at some pretty big mountains, and I know You can see them. Please help me to keep my eyes on You, instead of the mountains. I believe You are bigger, stronger, able, and willing to make a way for me. As You renew my mind by Your Word, help me to remove the word "but" from my vocabulary. I do not want to be double-minded. I want to operate in the kind of faith that moves mountains. I am training my mind to remain fixed on You. I know that You are answering my prayers. I am growing day by day, and I'm feeling stronger as I make this journey. Thank You for carrying me, leading me, and challenging me to follow You into the Promised Land. In Jesus' name, Amen.

# The Promised Land
## Part 3

Hey, friend!

I can't believe I made it to the Promised Land! Life is good here—not always easy, but definitely good. You don't have to tell any lies here! No cover-ups! Imagine that! This place is the real deal!

Hope you can join me soon!

Peace, freedom, and contentment

P.S. Check out these pictures! They are A-1 authentic!

## Snapshots of the Promised Land

Hi, I'm Deanna.

For me, walking into the Promised Land meant freedom. I wasn't in bondage to drugs, alcohol, sex, or even recovery groups. I could spend beautiful weekends with my husband and kids, and it didn't involve bars, clubs, alcohol, drugs or bad relationships.

Living in the Promised Land has also meant walking with Jesus and experiencing His amazing power and presence. My loving Savior will never leave or forsake me. He has given me a future and a hope. He has equipped me with everything I need to be more than a conqueror. His victorious life is so indescribably wonderful that I can't even compare it to all the junk I experienced in Egypt. He's so different than some groups that might label me a loser or an addict for the rest of my life. Praise God, I am living the abundant life that Jesus promised in John 10:10. Life only gets better and better from now until eternity.

I praise God that I haven't used or abused since September 13, 1997. But life in the Promised Land is not a perfect life. I mess up and get mad at my husband or kids. The devil wants us to backslide all the way to Egypt. But when I mess up, I simply say, "I'm truly sorry." I refuse to let the sun set on my anger. I turn to the promises of God and the glory ahead. And I keep walking. In the Promised Land, I am a saint who sometimes sins. I'm no longer a sinner who is sometimes a saint.

In a way, the walk from Egypt to the Promised Land turns you inside-out. In Egypt, you are so self-centered that ME is all that matters. Nobody can have a lasting, meaningful relationship in Egypt, because true intimacy doesn't exist when we only care about ourselves. Thankfully, it's just the opposite in the Promised Land. I no longer care about my own will. Instead, I want the will of my Father. I have made incredible friendships with other people who are focused more on God than on themselves. And the more I'm concerned about God and others, the more God opens the floodgates of heaven and pours incredible blessings and happiness on ME! But I've learned that these blessings are not just for me. I'm blessed so that I can be a blessing to others. The more I give, the more He blesses me.

My greatest joy living in the Promised Land comes from walking with Jesus, knowing He has a purpose for me, and enjoying intimate relationships with my family and friends. I also receive so much joy when Jesus works through me to bless other people with His amazing love. I don't care what troubles the future holds. I am walking with Jesus, so it is well with my soul. He is the Good Shepherd who will never forsake me.

Hi, I'm Michelle.

Well, I'm out of the recovery program, and although you might think everything is easy here, it's not. Actually, it's confusing at times. How am I supposed to act? What will I do now? How is this "new me" supposed to relate to people from my past? These are some of the questions I find myself asking almost daily. I'm such a different person today, but everyone around me is the same.

I have to be honest. A lot of times, I am tempted to go back to who I was before. It's easier to return to what is familiar; to an addiction, a behavior, a coping skill, a relationship, a mindset, a well worn path. We want to go back to what feels comfortable and safe. It's easy for me to pick up the victim role again, for me to pick up that bottle again, or for me to return to that coping behavior when things get a little too real. At least back then, I knew who I was. It had been established many years ago that I was a dysfunctional, abused, addicted trouble-maker. I knew how to use destructive habits to temporarily cope with just about anything.

But here in this new place, it's difficult to know who I am. Sure, my identity is in my Father God. Now I have tools to handle problems without turning to past strongholds. But how do I relate to others? How do I deal with people who are trapped in a lifelong addiction mentality? How do I live a lifestyle that is holy and pleasing to God? How do I respond to people who treat me as if I am still the same old addict? I have so many questions and insecurities. But I keep holding onto the same, simple truth God gave me when I left for residential treatment: "Trust me." This is where I find the strength to keep moving forward. I trust Him!

As I take more and more steps away from the person I was, and as I walk into the Promised Land, God provides for me and loves me in unfathomable ways. He gave me a great family that took me in as their own when I graduated from my program. God has totally used them to restore the brokenness from my biological family. I never thought this restoration was possible. Each day, God gives me the ultimate desires of my heart! He has provided for my needs, just as He sent fresh manna to the Israelites each morning. He is teaching me to trust Him instead of myself, and to stop trying to control every circumstance.

Once, when I was feeling down, Deanna said, "Things might seem difficult right now, but you always have three choices: 1) You can turn back to what you left behind; 2) You can stay where you are and later wonder why you just can't seem to put this pain behind you; or 3) You can press further into the Promised Land."

I have decided to press on. Moving forward is always the best. Even the worst day walking a tough road with God is way better than the best day without God. I have no intention to remain the same for the rest of my life. I aspire to look more and more like Jesus, the One who bought my life with His own blood. So even though I may not know what the future holds, I trust God's promise of a beautiful destiny.

Hi, I'm Jennifer.

Here's a warning from personal experience: Egypt is closer than you think--no matter where you are walking today. God rescued me from an Egypt of drugs, alcohol, and adultery over ten years ago. I had found my place in ministry and I was really enjoying life with Jesus in the Promised Land. But I experienced a time of loneliness that Satan exploited. He tempted me with a man whom I should never have looked at twice. Instead of rejecting those temptations, I started imagining what it might be like to slip on over to the dark side. Soon, I was having this strange conversation with God. I said to Him, "I know that this is not what You want for me. I even realize that this temptation will have bad consequences. But God, I just need You to back off right now. I'm lonely, and I'm going to do this."

Unfortunately, that's exactly what I did. I gave into the lust and the desire. What followed was an avalanche of guilt, shame, emotional pain, damaged relationships, and my ability to serve God with my whole heart. It's only by God's grace that I didn't relapse into drugs and alcohol. There's a Scripture that describes what happened to me:

"When an evil spirit comes out of a person, it goes through dry places looking for a place to rest. But it doesn't find any. Then it says, 'I'll go back to the home I left.' When it comes, it finds the house swept clean and in order. Then the spirit goes and brings along seven other spirits more evil than itself. They enter and take up permanent residence there. In the end the condition of that person is worse than it was before." (Luke 11:24-26)

When I stepped back into Egypt, I was filled with seven demons who were more terrible than anything I'd known before. I'm so mad at Satan! Neither my loneliness nor temptation was nearly as bad as the pain that tormented me and the chains that dragged me back to Egypt. I had made a horrible, horrible mistake.

After a long time, God has helped me to acknowledge my sinful lifestyle and begin to deal with it. But don't think that it's easy to slide back into Egypt and come out again without serious consequences. It's not like a holiday weekend where you have some fun and then return to life as normal. I'm still finding my way back to the place where I should be. I've lost ground, but at least I'm headed in the right direction again.

*Hi, I'm Cris.*

*I am amazed at how God has restored my innocence. What a miracle! This used and discarded girl – this dirty girl who felt she was bad because of all the bad that had been done to her – has been given a clean start. The tears I shed today for that little girl are no longer tears of pain. They are tears of thankfulness and joy for the tender miracle of restoration that Jesus has done in my heart. Imagine that – God has restored my innocence! I was robbed of my childhood, but today I feel like a little girl in a woman's body, dancing with my twirling skirt in my Heavenly Father's presence. Can you see how pleased He is? Watch Him embrace me in His loving arms. He gives me a kiss on the cheek and tells me how pleased He is with me. He loves me so much!*

*This is my inheritance, and nobody can ever take it away from me. I remember how close I was to losing my inheritance in Egypt. I remember it as if it were yesterday. But now that my restoration is behind me, God has called me to go back into the belly of the whale where I came from. I find joy being with the ones Jesus loves so dearly – the misfits, the untouchables, the addicts, the hopeless sinners. God has not called me to change, fix, or save anybody. He simply has called me to love them. I'm walking with Jesus, who cares so dearly for broken people.*

*It's awesome how God takes the junk from our past and actually transforms it into a tool for righteousness. He's using my past experiences to help others today, because the power of the Promised Land is much stronger than the power of Egypt. This is the testimony of my victorious life as a child of God in the Promised Land.*

# The Few Who Made It
## Part 3.1

While relaxing at the beach one day, I pondered the things of God. For a long time, I sat watching surfers; their victories and defeats. God revealed to me some very cool spiritual insights.

As the waves crashed and the surf pounded, a young couple wearing surf gear waded into the water to encounter the Big Kahuna. They swam out and got tossed around. No, tossed around is not an accurate description. I would have to say that the woman got pummeled by the waves. She was choking and gasping for air. They tried again, but the same thing happened; they kept getting beaten back by the waves. They tried to get out into the deep waters where others were surfing but the woman couldn't make it past the big waves near the shore. After several tries, she looked defeated. I saw her talking to her companion. She was pointing to a place further up the beach. It appeared to me that he wanted to stay at the same location, but she kept shaking her head and pointing down the beach. He eventually gave in to her pleas. I chuckled to myself. He saw failure, while I saw her admirable attempts.

I then turned my attention on the surfers who were able to swim past the big waves along the shore. They, too, were tossed about. They struggled to hold on to their boards. It looked like exhausting, incredibly hard work, just to stay out there. A few of them managed to get up on their boards and ride for a short-lived victory. I wondered if they thought all that work was worth it.

Then, I noticed something interesting. Some surfers were floating out in the big waves with ease. They didn't struggle like the other surfers who wore themselves out, by fighting the ocean. These surfers just tucked their heads down when the big waves came, and let mountains of water roll right over them. They didn't fight the waves or muscle their way through them. Their technique was graceful and rhythmic. They glided up and down, in and out, over and over. They were saving their strength for the important part of surfing, where they actually stood up and rode the waves. I thought to myself, *if I were a surfer, that's how I would hope to do it.*

## The Parable of the Surfer

Then it became so clear to me. I had a revelation that I'll call the Parable of the Surfer. It's a parable of possession and authority. In the ocean of life, too many of us get beat up and tossed out before we even discover what we're looking for. We're reaching for the prize, when suddenly, we find ourselves exhausted, frustrated, and defeated. We don't know what hit us. We only hope to get out where the more advanced surfers are riding the exhilarating and amazing waves of life. We wish we could get to places where others have gone.

The inexperienced surfers may be good swimmers. They may be strong. But all of their efforts get them nowhere. They waste so much energy just laboring and laboring! They encounter the same waves as the experts, but they become tired, trying to bear the weight of the ocean on their own shoulders. They fight, work, and push to get to where they are. They know they could get so much further….but how? Others can do it. Why can't they? Perhaps they lack the training or right equipment.

I thought about my walk with God. I'm thankful that in recent years, more of the big waves of life are rolling right over me. When I was a baby Christian, I had little knowledge of God's authority and the power of the Holy Spirit. The challenges of life really tossed me around and spit me out. I didn't even dream of riding the waves. Then, I matured a little, and learned to muscle through some of the challenges. I saw some victories, but boy, was I tired. And I hadn't even encountered the really big waves yet!

Slowly, God showed me how to cling tightly to Him. I knew that He would keep me safe from every crashing wave of life that could destroy me. He is my tower of refuge and strength. Through prayer and fasting, I can be safe amidst the turbulence of life. I can come out on top of the wave! As I sat there on the beach, the surfers became a clear picture to me of life in the Promised Land. They show the difference between those who embrace the promises and full authority of God….and those who don't.

> *Therefore whoever hears these sayings of mine, and does them, I will liken*
> *him to a wise man who built his house on a rock. And the rain came down,*

*and the floods came, and the winds blew and beat on that house. And it did not fall, for it was founded on a rock. (*Matthew 7:24-25, NKJV*)*

*So that we no longer may be infants, tossed to and fro and carried about by every wind of doctrine, in the dishonesty of men, in cunning craftiness, to the wiles of deceit.(*Ephesians 4:14, NKJV*)*

## Tribulation Produces!

God has a lot to say about contentment. We often lose our contentment during trying times. It's easy to be content when you're in good health, there's plenty of food on the shelf, and gas in the car, right? But during the hard times, the true colors of our faith come to light.

The scriptures talk about the benefits of tribulation. We spend too much time and energy trying to figure out the source of our tribulation. John 16:33 says: "In the world you *will* have tribulation." Sometimes things just are. Like they say, "It is what it is."

> *More than that, we rejoice in our sufferings, knowing that suffering produces endurance and endurance produces character, and character produces hope, and hope does not put us to shame, because God's love has been poured into our hearts through the Holy Spirit who has been given to us.* Romans 5:3-5, ESV

This is incredible! Paul says we rejoice in suffering! *Yeah, right!* If that's not your idea of fun, the word for "rejoice" in the original Greek translation actually means more than just being happy. It also means "to wish" or "desire" suffering. Now, doesn't that sound sick? If a friend hears you talk about wanting tribulation and suffering, they'll likely take you in for counseling. But the Bible says that some forms of suffering are good for us.

We also know from the Bible that "The spirit is willing but the flesh is weak." (Matthew 26:41) Come on, if we are honest, who likes to suffer? Why is it that we don't hear much preaching on identifying with the suffering of Christ? Material prosperity is so much easier to swallow than the message of suffering. Sure, God desires our spiritual, mental, and physical prosperity. But total prosperity also involves difficult things like fasting and giving up something you want in order to give someone else what they need! Who wants to talk about the price of losing our life to gain it? That would mean I would have to give some things up. I might have to be uncomfortable. I might have to give of myself and my finances. I'll have to relinquish my right to be "queen of the universe" and trust God that He is able to hold it all in balance.

## God's Hotel

I checked you in again last night, My child,
Cuz it hurt Me so bad to see you out there, running wild.
All tired and sucked up you appeared to Me,
But put a mirror in front of you and you can't even see
That you number among the walking dead,
Sores all over your body, confusion in your head.
Jail is not the place you want to be,
But it's "My hotel" where I can work on thee.

You see, you weren't just arrested.
You were rescued from yourself.
I had to bring you back here
To put your drug use on the shelf.
Give you some rest, some food, and some talk.
Encourage you and love you before I let you walk.

Don't be like a mule that's led around by a bit.
Just listen to My warnings and I can help you quit.
This could be the last time you have to come into this place.
Just listen to Me, the Creator of all, with tears upon My face.

*By Leisa Lopez*

So, how can we reach a point where we find joy in tribulation, just as an experienced surfer finds joy the big waves? How can we focus on the beautiful things God is doing through suffering, instead of focusing on our own short-sighted, selfish desires?

In John 15, Jesus uses the metaphor of a vine. Some branches are cut off and burned because they produce no fruit, and other branches are pruned to produce more fruit. God uses difficult times to prune us, to produce more spiritual fruit in and through our lives.

144

*I am the real vine, and my Father is the gardener. He breaks off every branch in me that does not bear fruit, and he prunes every branch that does bear fruit, so that it will be clean and bear more fruit. (John 15:1-2)*

*My friends, consider yourselves fortunate when all kinds of trials come your way, for you know that when your faith succeeds in facing such trials, the result is the ability to endure. (James 1:2-3)*

Going back to the Parable of the Surfer, Charles Spurgeon, a man of God from the nineteenth century, understood how the mighty ocean relates to our knowledge of God's power and authority. He said:

*"Those who navigate little streams and shallow creeks, know but little of the God of tempests; but those who 'do business in great waters,' these see His 'wonders in the deep.' Among the huge Atlantic waves of bereavement, poverty, temptation and reproach, we learn the power of Jehovah, because we feel the littleness of man."[1] – Charles Spurgeon*

## Patience Versus Perseverance

Patience is different than perseverance. Patience is waiting *with contentment*, which is much different than just waiting. When we surrender our situation to God, we can wait with contentment, knowing that He will work all things for our good. We have to trust and have faith in Him! God cannot fail!

Perseverance, on the other hand, involves more than just waiting with contentment. Perseverance involves *fighting the battle with faith while we wait*, knowing that help is on the way. Perseverance takes longer to develop. We can have patience for a week or a month, but if a trial persists for a long time (like when a child is born with special needs, or a spouse has a terminal illness) it takes a lot more than patience to endure. It takes perseverance.

When our trials seem to last forever, when months turn into years, that is a test of our perseverance. When the enemy attacks us with thoughts of doubt and hopelessness; it's a test of our perseverance. We must learn to fight the good fight of faith during these tests. Why? Because of the *hope* it produces.

*Endurance produces character, and character produces hope. (Romans*

---

1 Charles Spurgeon, *Morning & Evening* (Wheaton, IL: Crossway Books, 2003).

5:4*)*

*Hope deferred makes the heart sick, but when the desire comes, it is a tree of life. (*Proverbs 13:12*)*

Hope is believing that God is working everything for our good–right now! Hope is believing that God loves us and is going to take care of us–right now! Hope is believing that we're in the center of God's will so we can have peace and joy–right now! Hope is believing that God is with us–right now, no matter what trial we may be going through.

It's a joy to be in the trenches of life with you; to pray and stand together when tribulation comes; to see the fruit being produced. God is working perseverance, patience, character and hope into each one of us through life's trials. He has an awesome call on our lives. He has placed a destiny before us.

Sometimes those trials appear in the waiting room of life. I'd like to share an amazing poem I received from a precious sister in Utah:

### Waiting

Desperately, helplessly, longingly, I cried.
Quietly, patiently, lovingly, God replied.
I pled and I wept for a clue to my fate,
And the Master so gently said, "Child, you must wait!"

"Wait? You say, wait?" My indignant reply.
"Lord, I need answers, I need to know why!"
Is Your hand shortened? Or have You not heard?
By FAITH I have asked, and am claiming Your Word.

"My future and all to which I can relate
Hangs in the balance, and You tell me to WAIT?"
I'm needing a "yes," a go-ahead sign.
Or even a "no" to which I can resign.

"And Lord, You promised that if we believe
We need but to ask, and we shall receive.
And Lord, I've been asking, and this is my cry
I'm weary of asking! I need a reply!"

Then quietly, softly, I learned of my fate

As my Master replied once again, "You must wait."
So, I slumped in my chair, defeated and taut –
And grumbled to God, "So, I'm waiting……for what?"

He seemed then to kneel and His eyes wept with mine.
And He tenderly said, "I could give you a sign.
I could shake the heavens, and darken the sun.
I could raise the dead, and cause mountains to run."

"All you seek I could give, and pleased you would be –
Would have what you want, but you wouldn't know ME.
You'd not know the depth of my love for each saint;
You'd not know the power that I give to the faint."

"You'd not learn to see through the clouds of despair,
You'd not learn to trust just by knowing I'm there.
You'd not know the joy of resting in Me–
When darkness and silence were all you could see."

"You'd never experience that fullness of love
As the peace of my Spirit descends like a dove;
You'd know that I give and I save…. (for a start)
But you'd not know the depth of the beat of My heart."

"The glow of My comfort late into the night
The faith that I give when you walk without sight.
The depth that's beyond getting just what you asked,
Of an infinite God, who makes what you have last."

"You'd never know, should your pain quickly flee,
What it means that "MY GRACE IS SUFFICIENT FOR
THEE."
Yes, your dreams for your loved ones overnight would come
true,
But, oh the loss! If I lost what I'm doing in you."

"So, be silent, my child, and in time you will see
That the greatest of gifts is to get to know ME.
And though oft may My answer seem terribly late,
My wisest of answers is still but to WAIT."

*By Mishcelle in Grand County Jail, Utah*

## Pick Me! Pick Me!

If we persevere, God can use our suffering for good in others' lives. The Bible says in Matthew 20:16 and Matthew 22:14 that many are called, but few are chosen. Have you ever wondered if there is some kind of formula for being chosen? I have often wondered why God would choose to bless me with such amazing opportunities to serve Him. I think the formula for me has been this: willingness + surrender + obedience + suffering + sacrifice + faith = being chosen.

Don't confuse your salvation with being chosen for ministry. Remember that your salvation is a free gift that Christ paid for by shedding His innocent blood on the cross. If you truly believe that Christ died for your sins and have confessed that to Him with an earnest heart, your salvation is secure.

Likewise, don't mistake ministry for doing good things in and through the church. Real ministry is taking what we have learned and applying it to our circumstances. Let me give you an example:

In writing this book, I spoke with my friend, Trish Hart. She was addicted to drugs for twenty-five years. During the four years she spent incarcerated in a California women's prison, Jesus Christ set her free. When she got out of prison, she wrote a book called, *You Are Never Alone* (Tate Publishing, 2007).[2] God opened the door for her to work for a growing company. The owner put her in charge of opening up a new department. She confessed to me that while interviewing people to fill the open positions, she took a step of faith and hired people who were wandering in the Wilderness; women who were molested as children; a man who was living in his car; two gay men; one young man who told her that he had tried to commit suicide.

From a business standpoint, you would want to hire people who were strong and stable, but she chose to offer a hand up to "the least of these." She gave them a job, and tried to love them like Christ loves her. She spreads a little "Word seed" throughout the day, and those people are thriving and doing a wonderful job for her! It didn't surprise me that the company is receiving even more opportunities than the owner ever thought possible. As a matter of fact, Trish just opened a second department bigger than the first, and her salary has more than doubled! She will be the first to tell you that God gets all of the glory! When you set aside your own agenda and put God's interest first expect increase!

When Trish asked God why those people had revealed the details of their lives in a

---

2 Trish Hart, in discussion with author, 2008.

job interview, she told me that God's answer was, "I led them to where mercy could be found." She wept, because she was happy to be at a place in her walk with God where He trusted her! Trish is a great example of someone who doesn't just see ministry as something that happens inside the four walls of the church.

Are you, or have you been called, to minister? *Absolutely.* Have you been chosen? *Yes!*

## Perseverance and Obedience

Obedience means not taking on that Wilderness mentality again—even when you blow it. Even when the enemy starts throwing lies in your face like*: Hey loser. You screwed up. Now you're all the way back at the beginning again. All this "God stuff" must not be working.* I've heard those lies just like you have. Don't believe them! Proverbs 24:16 says, "Though I fall seven times I will get up." Obedience means standing back up and walking forward. You may not feel like it, but do it anyway. Sometimes courage is the art of doing it scared!

## How Much Are You Worth?

We need *His* vision for our lives. We must see ourselves as *He* sees us. We cannot think of ourselves more highly than we ought….but neither should we see ourselves as anything less than joint heirs to the throne of grace. We are royalty! Our worth was determined by the price that Christ paid for us. His life blood shows the value of your life and mine—*wow!* Chew on that for a moment. We are daughters and sons with an incredible eternal destiny in the presence of the King of Kings. We don't belong to the prince of this world! We are members of heaven's kingdom!

Vision and obedience are easier to keep in perspective when we understand our identity. The few who make it to the Promised Land understand who they are in Christ.

## Stop And Think!

How are you surfing? Are you struggling with the circumstances of your life?

_____

_____

_____

_____

_____

What trials have produced patience in your life?

_____

_____

_____

_____

How have you had to persevere?

_____

_____

_____

_____

Describe your feelings about suffering:

_____

_____

_____

_____

_____

In what areas of your life is God calling you to obey?

_____

_____

_____

_____

_____

How do you see yourself? How does that image compare with how God sees you?

_____

_____

_____

_____

_____

## Prayer Point

God, I have been washed under by the waves of life. I would like to see how the situations in my life have produced godly character in me. Please show me, Father, how I can persevere. I believe that You, Lord, have a purpose for me. I want to walk fully in the Promised Land. I want to see things the way You see them. Help me, Lord, to be more willing, surrendered, obedient, faith filled, able to withstand, and even appreciate, suffering. Lord, help me die to my selfish nature that does not want to lay things down, so that You can replace my desires with something more valuable. I want to walk the narrow road that few find. I will need Your help to find my way. Thank You, Father, that You have brought me this far and that You do not plan to leave me here.

# Crossing the River
## Part 3.2

After wandering in the desert for forty years, the Israelites were more than ready to conquer the Promised Land. So, they camped beside the Jordan River, at the edge of the wilderness. But Moses, who was now 120 years old, never actually walked into the Promised Land. Here's what happened:

> *Moses went up from the plains of Moab to Mount Nebo, to the top of Mount Pisgah east of Jericho, and there the Lord showed him the whole land....Then the Lord said to Moses, "This is the land that I promised Abraham, Isaac, and Jacob I would give to their descendants. I have let you see it, but I will not let you go there." So Moses, the Lord's servant, died there in the land of Moab....The people of Israel mourned for him for thirty days in the plains of Moab. Joshua son of Nun was filled with wisdom, because Moses had appointed him to be his successor.* (Deuteronomy 34:9)

Joshua, not Moses, led the Israelites into their destiny. God equipped Joshua with wisdom for this important job as Moses' successor.
*The Devil and the Mountaintop*

Moses' mountaintop experience with God reminds me of a mountaintop experience Jesus had ... but it wasn't with God.

> *The Spirit led Jesus into the desert, where he was tempted by the devil for forty days ... The devil took him to a high place and showed him all the kingdoms of the world in an instant. The devil said to him, "I will give you all the power and glory of these kingdoms. All of it has been given to me, and I give it to anyone I please. So if you will worship me, all this will be yours." Jesus answered him, "Scripture says, 'Worship the Lord your God and serve only him.'"* (Luke 4:1-8)

This story is a warning for all of us. God is not the only one who takes us to the mountaintop. He is not the only one interested in our destiny. We must be very careful to use discernment, a gift of the Holy Spirit, to determine if the "Promised Land" we desire is from God or from the devil.

Let me tell you about one of my own mountaintop experiences that required discernment. It happened after my recovery, when I had already spent several years serving in ministry. I believed that I was right where God wanted me to be at that particular time. And in many ways, I was. A lot of great ministry opportunities were opening up for me. My platform was expanding to the regional and national level. I was in a realm I had not experienced before, and God was showing off His power and glory all around me. Or, so I thought.

I was cruising right along and watching great things happen. The time came for me to consider moving into a more prominent position with a particular ministry. I traveled out of town to meet with the ministry's national and regional directors to determine where I would fit into the "big picture" of the organization. I was feeling pretty good about the direction things were going.

After meeting for several hours and not coming to a place of resolution, we decided to break until the following day, to pray and seek God's direction for my future in the ministry. I returned to the hotel, feeling tired and a bit frustrated. Things were not going as smoothly as I had anticipated. My hotel was kind of a dump. I could hear the sound of fighting and parties. My room was cold and smelled like stale cigarettes. The weather outside was as hazy and dreary as my mind. I took out my Bible. In my spirit, I began to dialog with God.

God whispered words into my heart. He reminded me that when the devil was tempting Jesus, he took Him to a mountaintop and offered to give Him the world. Then God said to me, "The devil has you at the top of a mountain. He's offering to give you so much, because you've come to believe that this ministry has provided and been everything that you wanted or needed."

I thought, "If that's true, then I've been deceived. I don't want what the devil has for me. But I don't really understand, because I've grown in my faith and I'm using the gifts that you've given me. I'm in this great place! Why would I want to lay all of this down?"

God said, "Because the devil has taken you to a high place and has offered to give you all this stuff."

"But it hasn't felt that way," I thought.

Then God said, "What have you got? You've gotten a platform. You've gotten validation. You have people stroking your ego. But have you *needed* me?"

"Gosh," I said. "Not really. I've had a great time. It's been lots of fun." I thought of all the abilities and talents I had been using for His glory. I thought of the hundreds of people who had said, "You are so amazing." My heart began to get heavy. I couldn't remember the last time I prayed, seriously prayed, for God's help and guidance.

Confusion still clouded my brain. "But how could all of this not be from You?" I asked. "Look at all the kingdom work that's been accomplished. Look at all the pastors and leaders I've helped. Look at how You've used me."

Then He said, "But have you used *Me* in the process?"

"Wow!" I thought. "What are you saying, Lord?"

"Deanna, if I were to take you home tonight, would you have accomplished your life's purpose?? Do you think this is it?"

I knew I hadn't. And a huge feeling of something like grief came over me.

## Good, Great, or God

I sat for a long time in that dark, cold hotel room, seeking God as He impressed His desires on my heart, mind, and soul. He led me to examine my ways and test them, to see which of three categories they fell into:

❖ Good

❖ Great or

❖ God

You see, I had done "good" things for God ever since I was a baby Christian. Then I matured, and began doing "great" things in ministry (in my own small estimation). But they weren't great in God's eyes, because I hadn't even done the one thing He had sent me to accomplish; to rely fully on Him. I was still performing; only now it was in the area of ministry. He showed me I didn't even *need Him* to do the things that I was doing!

*You will succeed not by military might or by your own strength, but by my Spirit. (Zechariah 4:6)*

As I sat at His feet, God spoke to me through many different thoughts, images, and Scriptures. This is what He said:

*You have experienced great things in ministry. But you need to be very careful. You will never succeed by your own might or strength, but only by MY spirit. (Zechariah 4:6) I am a jealous God. You are to have no other gods before Me, including yourself. Beware of using the talents I've given you to steal My glory. Any great things you experience are not a result of your own efforts, but of Mine, so you have no reason to boast. (Ephesians 2:9) Many people get stuck in the great stuff and never experience the GOD stuff. The God things I call you to do will take you outside of your comfort zone, causing you to lean more on Me. You cannot do God things in your own strength. 'If the Lord does not build the house, the work of the builders is useless.' (Psalms 127:1) So My question is this, Deanna: Do you want the good things, the great things, or the God things for your life?*

For me, the answer to His question was obvious. I wept for the pain of His discipline, the reality of how off-track I had gotten, for the hit to my ego, for the thought of facing these spiritual leaders and telling them I had been wrong. But I knew this was the good and right thing to do. My sacrifice to God was a humble and broken heart. (Psalms 51:17)

The next morning, I went to my leaders and said, "I'm sorry. I've wasted your time. I need to give up this platform. I went to the top of the mountain. The devil showed me what I could have, and it's not what Lord wants me to have. So I don't want it."

They graciously accepted my resignation from a position that didn't even exist yet–funny how that worked out. Tearfully, I left that meeting wondering where in the world God was taking me. I had so many uncertainties, but one thing I knew for sure: I would never settle for the deceit of the GREAT THINGS when I could instead wait patiently for the GOD THINGS in my life.

## They Who Wait Upon the Lord....

I hope and pray that you will be patient as the Lord opens the way for you to walk into your Promised Land destiny. It doesn't happen overnight! Our enemy, Satan, may take you to the mountaintop and promise you a quick, easy, and glamorous route to your destiny. But don't take it! God's way may be slower, but it is infinitely better.

> *But those who wait upon God get fresh strength. They spread their wings and soar like eagles, they run and don't get tired, they walk and don't lag behind.* (Isaiah 40:31, MSG)

After I turned down Satan's mountaintop offer, God slowed me down for the next few years. He taught me so much about loving Him and loving my family. I spent a lot of time just pressing into Him and sitting at His feet. I learned from Him and His Word. I learned how much better it is to "be" a daughter of Jesus than it is to "do" a lot of busy work for Him. "Being" is better than "doing."

It's like the story of Mary and Martha from the Bible. Mary liked to sit at Jesus' feet and learn from Him, while Martha was always cooking, cleaning, and doing busy work for Jesus. One time, Martha got mad at Mary for not helping with the work. That's when Jesus rebuked the busy sister.

> *"Martha, Martha," he said. "You worry and fuss about a lot of things. There's only one thing you need. Mary has made the right choice, and that one thing will not be taken away from her." (Luke 10:41-42)*

I was learning how to be more like Mary; to stop finding worth in the things I achieved for God. Instead, I began to find worth in the fact that Jesus loves me and that I can sit at His feet and adore Him. In time, God gave me many wonderful things to "do" for Him, and today I have ministry opportunities more incredible than those Satan offered me. But all that busy work doesn't define me. And I can't do anything to earn God's approval or love. What could little ol' me do that the Lord and Master of the Universe needs or wants? But there's one thing He *does* want from each one of us more than anything, and that's our obedience, devotion, and love.

You are not defined today by your accomplishments, your looks, your wealth, or your image. What defines you is simply the fact that Jesus loves you, He chose you, He died for you, and He wants you to be in His family. You are a child of the King! That's the best reward of living in the Promised Land. Nothing else comes close to it.

## Stop And Think!

How have you been running on a performance treadmill?

_____

_____

_____

_____

What things do you feel keep you busy, rather than sitting at Jesus' feet?

_____

_____

_____

_____

How can you get into position for the "God" things?

_____

_____

_____

_____

Describe how you feel about letting go of positions that may simply provide validation.

_____

_____

_____

_____

_____

STOP & THINK

## Prayer Point

God, I want to make sure that I am in Your perfect will for my life. I don't want to just run on a hamster wheel of busyness and miss what You have designed for me. Please order my steps. When I have simply performed so that others can see how talented or valuable I am, –show me that I can rely on You for these feelings of adequacy. Lord, if I have taken a position that I now feel is not from You, please give me the strength to set it down. Then both I and the person You want in that role can be where You want and need us to be. I do not want to settle for believing that the devil has given me the world, when Your plan is so much greater for my life. Please give me wisdom to see what You have for me, Lord. Amen.

# Into Your Destiny
## Part 3.3

*Joshua sent two spies from the camp at Acacia with orders to go and secretly explore the land of Canaan, especially the city of Jericho. When they came to the city, they went to spend the night in the house of a prostitute named Rahab... Before the spies settled down for the night, Rahab went up on the roof and said to them, "I know that the Lord has given you this land. Everyone in the country is terrified of you. We have heard how the Lord dried up the Red Sea in front of you when you were leaving Egypt... The Lord your God is God in heaven above and here on earth. Now swear by him that you will treat my family as kindly as I have treated you, and give me some sign that I can trust you. Promise me that you will save my father and mother, my brothers and sisters, and all their families! Don't let us be killed!"*
*(Joshua 2:1, 8-13)*

I love this story of Rahab. She was the lowest of the low – a prostitute in a wicked, idol-worshiping nation. But look how noble she becomes in this moment of crisis! You don't see her saying, "I'm just a prostitute. I have nothing to live for. I can never change. Just let me die with all the others." No way! First, she makes an incredible profession of faith: "The Lord your God is God in heaven above and here on earth." This bold statement goes against everything she had been taught ever since she was a child. Like us, Rahab was the child of a godless culture. It's not easy for people to break from the herd, but amazingly this woman did it. And then she cries out for salvation. Now this is a woman who understands God's calling to a higher destiny!

That's not all. Later in the Bible, Rahab is praised for being one of the most godly and faithful people in all of history:

> *It was faith that kept the prostitute Rahab from being killed with those who disobeyed God, for she gave the Israelite spies a friendly welcome.* (Hebrews 11:31)

> *It was the same with the prostitute Rahab. She was put right with God through her actions, by welcoming the Israelite spies and helping them to escape by a different road.* (James 2:25)

Isn't that awesome?! Every citizen of Jericho may have labeled Rahab as a dirty prostitute without hope of ever lifting her head out of the gutter. But somehow, she found the courage and strength to believe differently. Today, she is enjoying a glorious eternal destiny in heaven as a beautiful daughter of the King, all because she chose to trust God and take Him at His Word.

## Life in a Box

In the beginning of this book, I told you the story of my childhood; how I believed the lies spoken over me that said I was nobody if I wasn't performing perfectly. Lies that said I had to look and act a certain way if I were "worth" anything. Lies that said all relationships were dangerous because everybody ends up hurting you in the end. These lies gave me a constant fear of rejection. They led me to sell my soul to people and to the devil; to numb my pain with drugs, alcohol, and sex; to tie myself to losers because I believed that *I* was a loser; to invite rejection and abuse because I thought that was all I deserved.

Maybe you've had similar thoughts about yourself. I call these thoughts our "box." Many of us have been shoved into a box by people close to us. These people have said, "You're not good enough. You'll never be worth my attention or affection. You don't deserve to be loved. You're stupid. You're ugly. You should know better. You should be ashamed of yourself."

You may have been told that you'll never get out of this box. The box is your destiny. You're told to stay in your little tiny box and live a little tiny life. So you live in the dark, lonely, depressing corner of your little box. Even after years have passed, and these people are no longer speaking words of rejection and condemnation over you, you still hear the voices in your head. Your tender heart becomes a database of negative words that cannot be changed. You are living the "box mentality" lie.

In order to fulfill our true, God-given destiny, we have to choose to come out of that box. Two simple words have really helped me in this process: "Not so!" First, let's get a clear picture of your box, so you can find the determination and strength to break out.

*"Not So!"*

> *Don't let the world around you squeeze you into its own mold, but let God remake you so that your whole attitude of mind is changed.* (Romans 12:2, PH)

When I was tucked away in the corner of my mental and emotional box, occasionally I'd hear God speak to my heart. It wasn't an audible voice; just a quiet thought or impression. But it was God's voice, all the same. He'd say something like, *Oh, Deanna, don't you see that I have created you for so much more? Don't you know that you were not meant to live this way? Don't you understand that I am your Daddy and the Creator of the universe? Surely I can give you wonderful things. Surely I can make you beautiful and new. You don't have to earn my love. Don't you realize that my incredible plans for your life are so much higher and better than your tiny desires?*

Meanwhile, I still heard the lies that kept me in my box. But I recognized the truth in God's voice, so gradually I began to listen to His voice more, and respond to the lies that had been spoken over me. With two simple words, God showed me how to fight the mental battle. As the lies were spoken in my mind, God gave me two simple words in response: "Not so!"

Jesus showed me that His words are truth (John 14:6), and that any words opposing Him must therefore be false. If Jesus believed I was loveable, and if He wanted to give me a beautiful destiny, the thoughts that kept me in my box must therefore be ugly lies. Gradually, God taught me how to take every thought captive and make it obedient to Christ (2 Corinthians 10:5), simply by speaking those two words: "Not so!"

So, when defeat and despair came over me like a black cloud, I made a conscious effort to listen to God's voice. Like a little ray of light in the darkness, I gradually became aware of my tiny box. I began to uncurl from my fetal position, and I even imagined myself standing up straight and tall. I no longer wanted to be surrounded by darkness and loneliness. I began to desire freedom from the box.

Then my desires and imaginations led me to the next step, which was fighting for freedom. But every time I stood up, I banged my head on the ceiling of the box. This rude interruption came in the form of bitter memories. "Give up, Deanna. This box is all you know. It's all you deserve. You aren't so stupid to think you can actu-

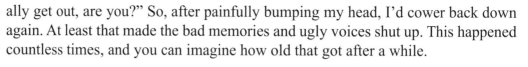

ally get out, are you?" So, after painfully bumping my head, I'd cower back down again. At least that made the bad memories and ugly voices shut up. This happened countless times, and you can imagine how old that got after a while.

One day, I decided I had had enough. I decided to fight past the point of pain and keep standing up. I thought maybe I'd even jump up a time or two. I rejected the lies and tried with all my might to believe the promises of God. I discovered that it still hurt to hit my head on the roof of my self-imposed prison, but at least it wasn't killing me. I could tolerate it. The hope of getting out of the box grew stronger and stronger. Success came by holding God's promises up to the lies of the enemy.

"Not so!"

## Breaking Out

We can become so used to bad situations when we've given up all hope. But once we taste the good life, we start to see our bad situation in a more realistic light. For me, the beauty of God's pure light gave me a despicable loathing for the darkness of my box. The more I read the Bible and the closer I walked with Jesus, the more I hated the lies of the enemy. I wanted out of the box! So I began to beat at the walls of my hard heart.

During that time, my head was full of conflicting emotions like hope and hopelessness, tears and laughter, faith and despair. That's what life is like between the Wilderness and the Promised Land. It's a confusing place, where the enemy is doing all he can to push you back. But I was close enough to feel the breeze blowing out from the Promised Land. I could smell its delicious fruit. So punching, scratching, kicking, and shouting, I fought with everything I had to break out of my tiny little box. I knew there had to be a way to get some light into the darkness of my heart.

Again, God spoke gentle words of encouragement to me during this time. He was saying:

> *My Word is a lamp unto your feet, a light unto your path.* (Psalms 119:105)

> *A good person's steps are directed by the Lord, and the Lord delights in his way.* (Psalms 27:23)

> *Trust in the Lord with all your heart. Lean not on your own understanding. Remember Him in all you do and He will show you the right way.* (Proverbs 3:5,6)

I used God's promises to strengthen and guide me. Gradually, I began to see little holes in my box. I watched as light began to shine in. And the more light I saw, the harder I fought to get out of the box completely.

I was growing spiritually and reading more of God's Word. I was stepping back from the people who would drag me back toward Egypt. I was beginning to get involved in ministry to others. On the outside, I was making small steps forward. But inside, I still struggled with the box of lies that threatened to squash my destiny. I could have lived like a hypocrite, with smiles and good performances on the outside, while secretly being paralyzed inside my box. Thankfully, God led me to deal with both the external *and* the internal darkness in my life.

## People Who Need People

Living inside of a box of lies can be extremely lonely. In the past, I had loved and trusted no one. I thought I was totally unlovable. I believed that whatever was to be gained from this rotten life had to be fought and won by my strength alone. Nobody else could be trusted. I had been deeply hurt by the people who were closest to me, so I strengthened my box by building fortress-like walls around my heart. I had strategies for keeping people at a distance or for sabotaging the relationship when I thought I might be hurt. But as the light began to shine on the lies in my box, I realized I couldn't live without people or relationships. I realized that the walls I had built to keep others out were actually walls that imprisoned me. I was punishing myself much more than others.

Again, God gave me a response to these lies about relationships. When I got fed up with people and wanted to put another brick on the wall around my heart, I'd hear those two simple words: "Not so!"

"You do need people," God was telling me. "You need to be accountable. You need to be taught. You need to take risks. You need to serve others. You need to allow others to serve you. It's not better to be alone than risk the pain of relationships."

> *Two are better off than one, because together they can work more effectively. If one of them falls down, the other can help him up. But if someone is alone....there is no one there to help him....Two men can resist attack that would defeat one man alone. (*Ecclesiastes 4:9-12*)*

Not only did I learn that I needed people, but I began to see how others needed me! As I began to see myself as a person of value who was precious in God's eyes (which was a huge step for me), God taught me that I was valuable to others, as well. He showed me how others needed the precious gifts He had placed in me. He wanted to use me to encourage, pray for, and minister to others.

His desire is the same for each of us. That's why we are called the "Body of Christ." A human body has so many unique members, and each one is needed to make the body complete. (1 Corinthians 12:12) No wonder our little tiny boxes are so lonely. We are not meant to live in solitary confinement. Isolation kills us! Without giving to others what God has placed in us, we shrivel away and die a slow death. That's what was happening to me. Like muscles atrophying from lack of use, I was withering away to nothing. I learned that to exercise these muscles, I had to both give to and receive from others. Listen to what God's Word says:

> *No one lights a lamp and then covers it with a washtub or shoves it under the bed. No, you set it up on a lamp stand so those who enter the room can see their way ... We're not hiding things; we're bringing everything out into the open. So be careful that you don't become misers ....Generosity begets generosity. Stinginess impoverishes. (*Luke 8:16-18, MSG*)*

It's possible to live inside a little tiny box and be stingy with what God has given us. I was shocked by the revelation that I was being stingy. I had never considered that before. Perhaps the most amazing revelation was that I was a gift–something of value! God had created me for a valuable purpose. These thoughts were new to me. As I continued to fight my way out of the box of "tiny living," I began to see things more clearly. Who was I to think that God makes junk? That's what I was saying to Him. "God, I know You made me, but I don't believe I have any value. There's nothing You put in me that's worth anything at all."

"Not so!"

Still the lies continued. "I never should have been born. I'm a mistake."

"Not so! Deanna is fearfully and wonderfully made." (Psalms 139:14)

My box fought to keep me contained. "You have no purpose in life. You'll never amount to anything."

"Not so!" God has said, "I know the plans I have for you, plans to prosper you and not to harm you, plans of a future and a hope." (Jeremiah 29:11)

I thank God that His "Not so" was victorious in the end. That's my story. But this victorious ending can also be *your* story, and I pray that it *will be*. You *will* break free from your little tiny box once you align your mind with Christ's….once you reject thoughts that don't agree with the Word of God….once you break down the walls of isolation….and once you see yourself as God sees you. He can blow your tiny box apart and God-size your life, once and for all!

## God is NOT in a Box!

The next question to ask yourself is this: do you have God in a box? As we walk further into the Promised Land, we will explore things that might limit God from doing all He said He would do. After all, Jesus said He gave us the Holy Spirit so that we could accomplish even greater miracles than He did. If that's not happening, we have to ask why.

My friend, Cris, once told me she enjoys the game of hide-and-seek that God plays with us. He has hidden the answers to our questions in His Word. He wants us to seek and find those truths. This pursuit is our key to victorious living. So, play a deeper game of hide-and-seek with God. Jesus said we should "seek first the kingdom of God." Let's press into God so that His kingdom will grow in and through us in ever increasing measure. This is the glory we experience in the journey out of Egypt, through the Wilderness, and into the Promised Land. Don't put God in a box. He has very big plans that involve you and me. Let's not underestimate the power of His kingdom.

Lord Jesus, let Your kingdom come here and now, as it is in heaven. We desire so much more of Your glory right here on earth. Your kingdom is so much bigger than our little tiny boxes. Let Your glory fill our hearts to overflowing and spill over into the entire world.

## STOP AND THINK!

How have you been living in a box?

_____

_____

_____

_____

_____

What mold were you squeezed into?

_____

_____

_____

_____

_____

How did you end up in the box? Who were some people responsible for the box?

_____

_____

_____

_____

What steps are necessary to forgive those people?

_____

_____

_____

_____

_____

What does it feel like in your box? How is God encouraging you to come of out the box?

_____

_____

_____

_____

_____

How have you underestimated God by putting Him in a box?

_____

_____

_____

_____

_____

What steps are you willing to take to break out of the box?

_____

_____

_____

_____

_____

What do you hope to find outside the box?

_____

_____

_____

_____

_____

## Prayer Point

Dear God, it's so dark, here in my box. I'm so lonely. I feel trapped, squashed, miserable, and hopeless. I want out so badly. Lord, please help me to break out of this tiny box I've been living in so I can live gloriously for You. I'd like to be free from all these things that have placed me, trapped me, and kept me in my box. Please help me, Lord.

Holy Spirit, reveal truth to me as I dare to answer these tough questions about what's keeping me from the life You want me to live. God, You said that You have a plan for me. Remove the obstacles and help me to reach that plan. Lord, I don't want to keep replaying the recordings in my head and my heart. I don't want to live inside of the fortress of walls I've created for my own safety. I want to trust You, God, and begin to allow people into my life. I want to grow, heal, and find true freedom.

Help me to fight, to stay strong, and to see clearly when You pierce the walls that make up my box. Father, You said that You have given me weapons of warfare for me that are not made by man, but that are mighty enough to destroy the strongholds of my box. I believe You can smash the walls down right here and now. In the matchless and mighty name of Jesus, Amen.

# Ultimate Victory!
## Part 3.4

### Raising the Dead

You've left Egypt *and* the Wilderness behind! Now you're standing in the Promised Land, and you have no intension of ever, ever going back. Congratulations! This is a time for celebration! Now that you're here, you probably expect life to be a whole lot better than it was in the past. And you should! You probably expect your life to be a lot more meaningful. And you should! You should expect God to work through you in power, to help people who are still trapped in that awful place you escaped from. God has big plans for you. He had big plans for you all along, even when you were a slave in Egypt. Now, it's time to begin walking into that incredible destiny.

But maybe you're wondering, "What *is* God's destiny for me?" Here is one of His most fantastic promises for you:

> *Truly, truly, I say to you, He who believes on Me, the works that I do he shall do also, and greater works than these he shall do, because I go to My Father. (*John 14:12*)*

These are the words of Jesus. Do you believe them? It's a bold claim–that we will do greater works than Jesus. Could that possibly be true for you today? I believe what the Bible says (most of the time).

Each year, I come before God to make a resolution. I specifically ask Him to reveal something new to me about Him, so that I can experience Him more. One year, I was walking the beach, having one of my deep, contemplative conversations with God. I asked God why most of us are not doing greater works than Jesus. His word said we would, so why, I wondered, aren't we experiencing those things?

I said, "God, if Jesus raised the dead, then why am I not raising the dead? How

must I change so that I can experience the things Jesus promised? Is it lack of faith, sin, or lack of understanding? What must happen for me to walk in that kind of power?"

At that moment, I heard God's voice in my Spirit. He said, "So, Deanna, are you saying that you've never raised the dead?"

Well, that was a shocking question. The answer was easy. "No, God. I think I would remember that one. It's not like I'd forget about Aunt Gertrude's funeral, when I prayed over her dead body and she jumped up dancing! It just hasn't happened to me."

He answered, "The reason you believe you have never raised the dead is because you are leaning on your own understanding. Your perception is different than Mine. My ways are not your ways. My ways are *higher* than yours."

By that time I was intrigued about what God was trying to show me. So, I pressed on. "Okay Lord, when have I raised the dead?"

Immediately, I saw a very clear picture of a young woman in my mind. I had been facilitating a recovery meeting when she came in off the streets. It was obvious she was struggling with an intense addiction. Thankfully, this young woman gave her heart to Jesus that night. As we said good bye, I gave her my phone number, in case she needed prayer or encouragement. A few days later, she called me and said that she was pregnant and had scheduled an abortion. By the tone of her voice, I knew she expected me to condemn her. Of course, I did not judge her, condemn her, or tell her what to do. I felt God simply wanted me to let her know I felt her pain. And I did! I knew she had some enormously difficult decisions to make. I let her know I would stand by her, regardless of the decision she made. Then, I asked if I could share with her the painful effects of my two abortions. It was okay with her, so I told her my story with transparency and vulnerability. As we talked, the similarities of our lives became evident. We were both walking the same path, although we stood that day in different places along the road. We cried together, and I let her know I would be praying for her and the baby, and that I would be available if she needed anything.

Later, she called me back to say she didn't keep her appointment for the abortion. She said that my words played over and over in her mind and she just couldn't get an abortion. I was so thankful. But she also said that she had decided to reschedule. This, she said, was her "only way out." I gave her the same words of assurance I'd stated earlier. I would be there for her and I would be praying for her.

The next scene in this story played out at my home church. We had a very large tent pitched while our new building was under construction. At the morning service, our pastors asked us to pray for good weather. It was pouring rain, and they wanted a good turnout for the evening service and guest speaker. We were going to pray away the storm. As I drove home after the service, with the rain pounding on my car, a tremendous sadness came over me. I seemed to hear God say, "Do not pray against this storm." I felt so conflicted, torn between what my pastors had said and what God was asking me to do. So, I decided not to pray against the storm. Then, I thought of this young woman. I felt like the pouring rain signified God's tears. I didn't understand what was going on, but I had a strong sense that the storm was tied to her situation.

The next day, the young lady called. She was agitated. The rain had prevented her from going to her rescheduled abortion that day. God's divine intervention had spared that baby. My part was very simple: obedience to not pray against the storm.

I didn't hear from this young lady for several weeks. Meanwhile, I was fervently praying and interceding for that precious baby. I later learned about a third time that this woman had scheduled an abortion, and that attempt also was thwarted. Then, one night, I was pleased to see her show up at the same recovery group where we had first met. In her arms was a beautiful, newborn baby boy. She approached me with tears in her eyes. Of course, I was bawling too, because I'm such a cry baby! She held the child out to me and asked if I wanted to hold him. Would I? Of course! As our tears showered down, she said she had named him after the angel Gabriel, because she knew the angels had been watching over him. We introduced little Gabriel to the whole group so they could rejoice, too. It felt so wonderful to play a small part in God's incredible plan.

God had answered my question: "When have I raised the dead?" when I remembered the story of Gabriel. Then God asked me again, "Do you still think you've never raised the dead in My name?" I had no words. He gently reminded me how that baby had been dead not once, not twice, but three times. At first I had thought God was crazy for saying I had raised someone from the dead, but in the end, He was absolutely right. This is a key to Promised Land living – not leaning on our own understanding.

> *Trust in the Lord with ALL your heart and do not rely on your own understanding. In all your ways acknowledge Him and He will make your paths smooth. (*Proverbs 3:4, 5)

# Be a Branch

*I am the vine, and you are the branches. Those who remain in me, and I in them, will bear much fruit; for you can do nothing without me. (*John 15:5*)*

Promised Land living is amazing and mind-baffling. This verse from John 15 tells us we *will* bear much fruit if we remain in Him. Yet, we complicate God's simple truth, redefining it according to our narrow vision. Usually, God's truth is so simple. He is the vine and we are the branches. How hard is that? In its simplest form, this says we are part of Jesus. He is the Lifesource. All nourishment comes from Him. We are an offspring–a branch connected to Him.

Let's look at more of the text:

*I am the real vine, and my Father is the gardener. He breaks off every branch in me that does not bear fruit, and he prunes every branch that does bear fruit, so that it will be clean and bear more fruit. You have been made clean already by the teaching I have given you. Remain united to me, and I will remain united to you. A branch cannot bear fruit by itself; it can do so only if it remains in the vine. In the same way you cannot bear fruit unless you remain in me. I am the vine, and you are the branches. Those who remain in me, and I in them, will bear much fruit; for you can do nothing without me. Those who do not remain in me are thrown out like a branch and dry up; such branches are gathered up and thrown into the fire, where they are burned. If you remain in me and my words remain in you, then you will ask for anything you wish, and you shall have it. My Father's glory is shown by your bearing much fruit; and in this way you become my disciples. (*John 15:1-8*)*

I have watched amazing transformation occur when people accept the reality of "vine living." Incredible life springs forth when people attach themselves to the vine. Miraculous changes occur. This is evidence of God's hand. As long as we submit our will to Him, He will move on our behalf.

On the other hand, I have watched people's lives fall apart when they go back to the lifestyle and habits of Egypt. "Those who do not remain in me are thrown out like a branch and dry up; such branches are gathered up and thrown into the fire where they are burned." This is exactly what happens to people who have been living in God's vineyard, active in the church, and connected to the Vine. I have seen it with my own eyes. I have watched their fruitful lives begin to dry up. All the good fruit of their lives is burned up if they do not continue to abide in Christ. They wake up and find themselves back in the dry and dusty wilderness.

Here's another amazing thing about the branches: All of my life, I wanted to be a part of something bigger than myself. I needed to feel connected. I wanted to know that I was accepted and valued by people who cared for me. This universal desire attracts many people to gangs. They simply want to belong to something bigger than themselves. That's why I hung out with the kids who were leading me to hell in high school. Everyone wants a family who will defend them; who they can defend. We want a reason to live. We want a purpose-driven life. We find that kind of life by staying connected to the body of Christ.

> *Let us not give up the habit of meeting together, as some are doing. Instead, let us encourage one another all the more, since you see that the Day of the Lord is coming nearer. (*Hebrews 10:25*)*

We cannot survive alone! Even animals in the wild know this. Instinctively, they huddle together, making it harder for the predator to snatch one of them away. In fellowship, we receive support, accountability, intercession, and corporate worship. We receive joy and intimacy in the fellowship of God's people. This is one of the greatest prizes of living in the Promised Land! We can have true and faithful friends….for the first time in our lives!

Naturally, this idea is foolishness to the people of the world.

> *For the message about Christ's death on the cross is nonsense to those who are being lost; but for us who are being saved it is God's power. The scripture says, "I will destroy the wisdom of the wise and set aside the understanding of the scholars." So then, where does that leave the wise?…. or the scholars?….or the skillful debaters of this world? God has shown that this world's wisdom is foolishness! For God in his wisdom made it impossible for people to know him by means of their own wisdom. Instead, by means of the so-called "foolish" message we preach, God decided to save those who believe. (*1Corinthians 1:18-21*)*

If we want to grow spiritually, we must be connected, submitted to, and serving God within a group of fellow believers. You don't want to be a lone ranger. Isolating yourself from the Body will cause you to shrivel up faster than anything else I have seen. You cannot stay in the Promised Land if you are cut off from the Body of Christ. Ultimate victory comes when we are being who we were created to be.

Ephesians 4:11 speaks of the earth being filled with His gifts. First Corinthians 12:29 tells us the Holy Spirit handed out gifts: to some apostles, prophets, evangelists, pastors, and teachers. We are a Body of many parts, but each part is equally important. You will remain in victory as you continue to be the gift that You were created to be. Don't ever forget the value that God says is in you. Don't worry about other people's gifts. Stay focused on your part, and allow God to use you for your purpose on earth.

God has used the Body of Christ to prune me and help me bear more spiritual fruit. When I'm connected with other believers, I don't slip unknowingly back into Egypt or stagnate in my walk with Christ. Fellowship builds in accountability and support that we can't get when we walk alone.

## More than Conquerors

Never, never believe that Promised Land living is "just getting by." Your destiny here is more than just surviving. It is a destiny of thriving and rising above the junk of life. It is a destiny of maintaining a positive, grateful attitude, despite the worst circumstances. It is the destiny of a conqueror!

> *In all these things we are more than conquerors through the one who loved us. (*Romans 8:37*)*

The chains and ropes of Egypt do not hold you anymore! You are free to conquer all the evil of this world – not in your strength, but in God's. I love the priceless spiritual wisdom that Neil Anderson gives on this topic:

> *"I have no desire to help anyone just cope with addiction. Freedom from the bondage of sin is the goal, and that will require knowing the truth about our new identity and position in Christ. Transformation also requires the renewing of our mind. Consider the ongoing battle for our mind and learn how we can tear down mental strongholds that have been raised up against the knowledge of God. (*2 Corinthians 10:5*) None of us can fix our past but by the grace of God we can all be free of its shackles. Jesus didn't come to give us coping skills. He came to give us life and make us new creations in Him."*[1] –Neil Anderson

## Until I'm Overtaken

Being overtaken by God is my heart's cry; to be fully consumed by His presence;

---

1 Neil Anderson and Mike Quarles, *Overcoming Addictive Behaviors* (Ventura, CA: Regal Books, 2003), 11-12.

to be the Proverbs 31 woman my Heavenly Husband can be confident in; to be the woman who operates in the fruit of the Spirit and continually has praise on her lips for God and others.

My desire is to be overtaken by God day by day, moment by moment. As I decrease and He increases, I don't' want people to see or hear me. I want to be so close to God that when I encounter people, they too, will have a God encounter.

I want to walk in a steady place, creating space in my life for God's power to come on me. (Acts. 1:8) I want to loose bonds, release burdens, and be a blessing in the lives of those around me.

I want to prepare myself (see Joshua 1 and 11) in ways the Holy Spirit reveals, pursue the presence of God, step into the water (see Joshua 3:3), and live fully in the Promised Land.

I don't want a mediocre experience, where I am only ankle deep in the things of God. I want to know the holy fire that refines me. This is my reasonable act of worship.

I want to find the treasures God has hidden for me. My goal is to press in, press on, and pursue the presence of God until I'm overtaken.

I've come too far. I can't go back to being a slave in Egypt. The years were wasted, my life frustrated. No wandering in the Wilderness anymore. I was designed for abundant, Promised Land living. I won't just remain; I'll continually change until' I'm transformed into the image of Christ. I'm a vessel of honor, lacking nothing of value. I am a trophy of grace. I hunger and thirst for righteousness. Let me be overtaken as I seek His face.

> *I wait for the Lord, my soul waits, and in His word I do hope. My soul waits for the Lord more than those who watch for the morning–Yes, more than those who watch for the morning. (Psalms 130:5, 6)*

## Don't Ever Stop Growing

I pray that you will continue to grow in your knowledge and understanding of God and His Word. With the tools you now have, you can pursue the promises of God for your life and the lives of those who you will meet. Our walk with God is a process. We are all learning to pursue the things of God, being transformed from glory to glory.

## Stop And Think!

How have you become convinced that you were designed for Promised Land Living? How do you feel about it?

_____

_____

_____

_____

What steps can you now take to make sure that you walk in victory and destiny?

_____

_____

_____

_____

Do you feel stronger and more valuable than before you started reading this book?

_____

_____

_____

_____

Explain it to yourself: Describe your feelings about your future with Christ as the center.

_____

_____

_____

_____

_____

STOP & THINK

## Prayer Point

God, thank You for allowing this time to share You with all of my precious readers, Your precious sons and daughters. As they close this book and move into the next portion of their journey in their relationship with You, remind them of the things they have learned from Your Word. You have given us the authority to call on heaven in our time of need, and I want to seal that promise right now. I proclaim that You will always be with them, for them, and in them. As the scriptures say; "Whoever shall call on the Name of the Lord Jesus Christ shall be saved and not put to shame!" Amen!

That's all for now, Daddy.

# Epilogue

*This year, in the process of writing this book, the Lord placed a burden on my heart to share the experience of being overtaken by the things of Him, rather than everything else. God has given me a vision and burden to show and share with women across the nation how to not only be overtaken once, but to live in that state of being. If your church would like to host a Destiny conference, where women or teens can be overtaken by the love of God, please contact me. It is my desire to see more of us enjoying the Promised Land–together.*

*Deanna Allen*

# Resource Center

### Additional resources to help you along your journey

If this book did what it was supposed to, some areas of your life were revealed where you can start a journey of healing. For example, in reading about my physical or sexual abuse, maybe you could relate. And while it hurts to admit it, you may desperately need some healing in this area. Or perhaps you have had an abortion and haven't grieved through the process of that choice yet. This section will provide some of my favorite books of healing. Some books are more general and will help heal several areas of life, while others target specific topics, such as abuse.

I also have recommended some of the most powerful resources in nationwide counseling and support groups. I've included ideas on finding a church that embraces the hurting person and adopts a philosophy of recovery.

This list is not exhaustive, nor is it necessarily a personal endorsement of the organizations listed. But this list starts a baseline of help in dealing with some of the issues brought up in this book. Please know that it's perfectly normal to be a little nervous, even scared, when you're first reaching out for help; but don't let that stop you. Sometimes the phone can seem like it weighs a thousand pounds, but be strong and courageous. Pick it up and call out for help. Make a decision today to do something for a positive change in your life or in the lives of those you love.

If you'd like prayer or encouragement in this step, I'd love to pray with or for you. Feel free to email or write to me. My contact information is located in the back of the book, following this resource center.

## Great Authors and Great Books:

**<u>Marty Angelo</u>**
*Once Life Matters,* Impact Publishing, 2006

**<u>Stephen Arterburn</u>**
I have particularly enjoyed the "Every Man" series. The books are not just for men, and the topics of sexual purity and healing are the clearest and easiest to apply and bring about change that I've found yet.

*Every Heart Restored*, WaterBrook Press, 2004

*Every Man's Battle*, WaterBrook Press, 2000

*Every Man's Marriage*, WaterBrook Press, 2001

*Every Young Man's Battle*, WaterBrook Press, 2009

*Addicted to Love: Understanding Dependencies of the Heart: Romance, Relationships and Sex*, Vine Books, 1991, 1996, 2003

**<u>David Berkowitz</u>**
*Son of Hope*, Morning Star Communications

**<u>John and Lisa Bevere, Messenger International</u>**
*Out of Control and Loving It; Giving God Complete Control of Your Life,* Creation House, 1996

*Be Angry But Don't Blow It: Maintaining Your Passion Without Losing Your Cool,* Thomas Nelson Publishers, 2000

*Driven By Eternity,* Time Warner Book Group, 2006

*Drawing Near,* Thomas Nelson Publishers, 2004

*Bait of Satan*, Charisma House, 2004

*Honors Reward, Faith Words*, Time Warner Book Group, 2007

*Under Cover*, Thomas Nelson, 2001

*Kissed the Girls and Made Them Cry*, Thomas Nelson Publishers, 2002

### Dr. Les Carter

*The Anger Trap: Free Yourself from the Frustrations that Sabotage Your Life*, Jossey-Bass, 2004

*The Anger Workbook*, Thomas Nelson Publishers, 1992

*Freedom from Depression Workbook (with Dr. Frank Minirth)*, Thomas Nelson Publishers, 1995

*Choosing to Forgive Workbook (with Dr. Frank Minirth)*, Thomas Nelson Publishers, 1997

### Henry Cloud and John Townsend

I have never picked up a book by these authors that didn't help me tremendously. A couple of my absolute favorites are:

*Boundaries*, Zondervan, 1992

*The Mom Factor*, Zondervan, 1996

*Safe People*, Zondervan, 1995

*Changes that Heal,* Zondervan, 1997

*Who's Pushing Your Buttons*, Integrity, 2004

### Ann Edenfield

*A Family Arrested*, available at www.wingsministry.org

### Joe Hare with Kathi Macias

*Changed at San Quentin...for Better or Worse,* AuthorHouse 2006

### Sharon A. Hersh

*Brave Hearts: Unlocking the Courage to Love With Abandon*, WaterBrook Press, 2000

### T.D. Jakes

*Woman Thou Art Loosed*, Destiny Image Publishers, 2006

*He Motions*, Putnam Adult, 2004

**Carol Kent**

*When I Lay My Isaac Down*, NavPress, 2004

*A New Kind of Normal*, Thomas Nelson Publishers, 2007

**Robert S. McGee**

*The Search for Significance: Seeing Your True Worth through God's Eyes*, Thomas Nelson Publishers, 2003

**Joyce Meyer**

Joyce is one of my all-time favorites. Any book by Joyce is a winner. These are just a few great places to start:

*Battlefield of the Mind*, Time Warner Book Group, 2002

*Be Anxious for Nothing*, Time Warner Book Group, 2002

*Approval Addiction*, Time Warner Book Group, 2005

*Eight Ways to Keep the Devil Under Your Feet*, Time Warner Book Group, 2002

*Enjoying Where You Are on the way to Where You're Going*, Time Warner Book Group, 2002

*How to Succeed at Being Yourself*, Time Warner Book Group, 2002

**Kathy Collard Miller**

*Why Do I Put So Much Pressure on Myself; Confessions of a Recovering Perfectionist*, Vine Books, 2000

**Frank Peretti**

*The Wounded Spirit,* Thomas Nelson Publishers, 2001

**Ray Pritchard**

*An Anchor for the Soul*, Moody, 2000

**David A. Seamands**

*Healing for Damaged Emotions: Recovering from Memories that Cause our Pain*, David C. Cook, 1991

*Freedom from the Performance Trap*, Victor Books, 1991

**Lennie Spitale**
*Prison Ministry: Understanding Prison Culture Inside and Out,* B & H Publishing Group, 2002

*Sentenced--Now What?: Relationships During Incarceration*

*Help! My Loved One is in Jail*

**David Stoop**
*Self-Talk*, Revell, 1996

**Kay Warren**
*Dangerous Surrender,* Zondervan, 2007

**Rick Warren**
*The Purpose-Driven Life*, Zondervan Publishing Company, 2002

**Kent Whitaker**
*Murder by Family: The Incredible True Story of a Son's Treachery and a Father's Forgiveness,* Howard Books, 2009

**H. Norman Wright**
*Always Daddy's Girl: Understanding Your Father's Impact on Who You Are*, Regal Books, 1989

*Making Peace With Your Past*, Revell, 1997

As I mentioned before, this list doesn't include all the tremendous resources that are available, but it's a place to start. Other resources have been integral in my recovery. Below are some ways you can go deeper into the areas of your struggles on your journey from recovery to destiny.

# Other Resources & Organizations

## American Association of Pastoral Counselor
9504 A Lee Highway
Fairfax, VA  22031
Phone:  703-385-6967

## Canaan Land Christian Center for Women
2377 County Road 65
Marburg, AL  36051
Phone: 334-365-9086
www.wrldnet.net

## Canaan Land Ministries (ministry to men)
P.O. Box 310
Autaugaville, AL  36003-0310
Phone: 334-365-2200
www.canaanland@bellsouth.net

## Celebrate Recovery
www.celebraterecovery.com

A Christ-centered 12-Step program that offers support and healing from all hurts, hang-ups, and habits. Global locations available. No referral necessary.

*Life Hurts God Heals*, Group Publishing, 2006 (youth version also available)

## Center for the Prevention of Sexual and Domestic Violence
1914 N. 34th Street
Seattle, WA  98103
Phone:  206-634-1903
Emergency: 800-562-6025

## Christian Association for Prisoner Aftercare (CAPA)
40 Hague Street, Suite 100
Detroit, MI 48202-2119
www.capaassociation.org

## Christian Growth Centers
P.O. Box 40
Hillsboro, NH  03244
Phone:  603-464-5555
Specializes in helping young people who have been battered and fragmented through broken homes, drugs, alcohol, etc.

## Dorcas House
Phone:  501-274-4022
Specializes in helping women and children who are victims of domestic violence.

## Daughters of Destiny
590 Hwy 105, Box 235
Monument, CO  80132-9125
www.impactlife.org/daughtersofdestiny
Provides Full Circle Ministry to incarcerated women and teen girls nationwide

## Ebenezer Outreach
www.ebrock.org
A Heart for Prison Ministry for the men and women behind the wall and beyond.

## Exodus International
P.O. Box 77652
Seattle, WA  98177
Phone:  206-784-7799
www.exodusintl.com
Equips and unites organizations to communicate freedom from homosexuality.

## Families in Crisis, Inc.
7320 Ohms Lane
Edina, MN 55435
Phone:  612-893-1883

## Holy Highway
Phone:  903-866-3300
Recommended for families with rebellious teenage girls.

## International Directory of Prison Ministries (IDPM)
http://prisonministry.net/directory/alphabetical/index.htm

## Kairos Ministries

130 University Park Drive, Suite 170
WinterPark, FL 32792
Phone: 407-629-4948
www.kairosprisonministry.org
Fellowship and ministry to incarcerated men and women, youthful offenders and female family and friends.

## Koinonia House National Ministries

PO Box 1415, Wheaton, IL 60187
Phone: 630-221-9930
www.koinoniahouse.org
(KHNM) seeks to implement our mission by creating relationships with churches, organizations and individuals seeking to fulfill the Lord's call in ministering to Christians coming out of prison through our Meet Me at the Gate® (MMATG) church program. Through this plan, we equip churches to execute a selection process, which effectively allows a local congregation to embrace at least one released inmate, our "Christian neighbor."

## Lord's Ranch

Box 700
Warm Springs, AR 72478
Phone: 870-647-2541
www.thelordsranch.com
A residential program for youth.

## Mercy Heart

P O Box 163783
Fort Worth, TX 76161
www.mercyheart.org
Founded in 1995, Mercy Heart has been there for families making adjustments when loved ones are incarcerated.

## Mercy Ministries of America

P.O. Box 111060
Nashville, TN 37222-1060
Phone: 615-831-6987
www.mercyministries.org
A residential facility, provided free of charge, for troubled young women and unwed mothers between the ages of thirteen and twenty-eight, who are willing to

commit six months to deal with life-controlling issues such as: pregnancy, drug and alcohol abuse, eating disorders, etc.

## Mike Barber Ministries
www.mikebarber.org

## NARPR – National Alliance for Radical Prison Reform
39 Pine Grove Road
Locust Grove, GA 30348
www.prisonministry.net/NARPR

## New Creations
Phone: 765-965-0099
Help for families with rebellious youth.

## New Horizons Ministries
1002 South 350 East
Marion, IN 46953-9502
Family and Christian character training.

## New Life
Phone: 800-NEW-LIFE
Counseling center and telephone crisis line.

## Parents Anonymous
Child Help USA
P.O. Box 630
Hollywood, CA 90028
A program for parents who already have or are afraid they might abuse their children.

## Prison Fellowship Ministries
44180 Riverside Parkway
Lansdowne, VA 20176
www.pfm.org

## Rapha
4351 Shackleford Road
Norcross, GA 30093
Phone: 800-383-HOPE
www.raphacare.com

Christ-centered, professional counseling for emotional and substance abuse, anxiety attacks, stress, unhealthy relationships, eating disorders, depressions, drugs, alcohol, suicidal tendencies, etc.

## Shelterwood
12550 Zuni Street
Westminster, CO 80234
Phone: 800-584-5005
www.shelterwood.org
A Christ-centered, residential-care facility providing counseling and support for teenagers and their families in a time of crisis.

## Speak Up For Hope
www.speakupforhope.org
Helping inmates and their families adjust to their "new normal"

## Teen Challenge International
P.O. Box 1015
Springfield, MO 65801
Phone: 800-814-5728
www.teenchallenge.com
Specializes in seeking spiritual solutions to addictive behavior patterns.

## Victim Offender Reconciliation Program (VORP)
Information and Resource Center
P. O. Box 1486
Asheville, NC 28802
(828) 318-2178
www.vorp.com
Victim-Offender Mediation Programs (VOMP), also known as Victim-Offender Reconciliation Programs (VORP) is a restorative justice approach that bring offenders face-to-face with the victims of their crimes with the assistance of a trained mediator, usually a community volunteer.

## Walter Hoving Home
P.O. Box 194
Garrison, NY 10525
Phone: 914-424-3674
Rebuilds lives shattered by drugs, alcohol, and other life-controlling problems.

**<u>Wings Ministry</u>**
2226 B Wyoming NE #130, Albuquerque, NM 87112
1-505-291-6412
www.wingsministry.org
The goal of the Wings Ministry is to connect spouses, caregivers, and children of inmates with the nurturing and supporting relationships of Christian people in local churches.

## Why Use Different Translations and Paraphrases of the Bible?

For two important reasons: first, the Bible was originally written using 11,280 Hebrew, Aramaic, and Greek words, but the typical English translation uses only around 6,000 words. Obviously, nuances and shades of meaning can be missed, so it is always helpful to compare translations.

Secondly, we often miss the full impact of familiar Bible verses, not because of poor translating, but simply because they have become so familiar! We think we know what a verse says because we have read it or heard it so many times. Then when we find it quoted in a book, we skim over it and miss the full meaning. Therefore, we have deliberately used paraphrases in order to help you see God's truth in new, fresh ways.

### Index of Abbreviations

| | |
|---|---|
| AMP | Amplified Bible |
| CEV | Contemporary English Version |
| ESV | English Standard Version |
| GWT | God's Word Translation |
| MSG | The Message |
| NASB | New American Standard Bible |
| NCV | New Century Version |
| NIV | New International Version |
| NKJV | New King James Version |
| NLT | New Living Translation |
| NRSV | New Revised Standard Version |
| PH | New Testament in Modern English (Phillips) |
| RSV | Revised Standard Version |
| TEV | Good News Bible: Today's English Version |
| TLB | The Living Bible |

## About the Author

Deanna Allen's personal story of recovery and redemption gives her a unique perspective and powerful voice to speak directly into the hearts of hurting and broken men, women and teens. Deanna is an effective, energetic and motivating communicator who is well known for inspiring audiences to their next level. Her passion is sharing and challenging others to be all they were created to be. She is the author of *The Son is Shining* and *Pathway to Serenity*. Over the past fifteen years Deanna's national speaking ministry has grown to include conferences, retreats, seminars, leadership development, mission organizations, church and youth events, She and her husband, Mitch live in northern California where they are raising five children, who range in age from four to twenty years.

Deanna is a member of AWSA (Advanced Writers and Speakers Association), COPE (Coalition of Prison Evangelists), CAPA (Christian Association for Prison Aftercare). Deanna has made multiple appearances on both radio and television shows and has been published in various newsletters, articles and anthologies. She is also a National Representative of Daughters of Destiny where she passionately speaks and teaches seminars inside of women's prisons around the country.

### Contact Information

To book Deanna for an upcoming event, contact Speak Up Speaker Services at www.speakupspeakerservices.com or call them at 1-888-870-7719.

To order additional books, teaching materials, and more information about Deanna and her ministry, visit her website at www.deannaallen.com.

To write to Deanna send mail to:
Deanna Allen
Abundant Place Ministries
PO Box 1244
Vacaville, CA 95696